Charles Foster Kent

A History of the Hebrew People

Volume 1

Charles Foster Kent

A History of the Hebrew People
Volume 1

ISBN/EAN: 9783337316655

Printed in Europe, USA, Canada, Australia, Japan

Cover: Foto ©Andreas Hilbeck / pixelio.de

More available books at **www.hansebooks.com**

A HISTORY

OF

THE HEBREW PEOPLE

A HISTORY

OF

THE HEBREW PEOPLE.

By CHARLES FOSTER KENT.

Vol. I.—The United Kingdom. With Maps.
12mo. *Net*, $1.25.

Vol. II.—The Divided Kingdom. With Maps.
12mo. *Net*, $1.25.

A HISTORY

OF

THE HEBREW PEOPLE

FROM THE SETTLEMENT IN CANAAN TO
THE DIVISION OF THE KINGDOM

BY

CHARLES FOSTER KENT, Ph.D.

ASSOCIATE PROFESSOR OF BIBLICAL LITERATURE AND HISTORY
BROWN UNIVERSITY

WITH MAPS AND PLANS

NEW YORK
CHARLES SCRIBNER'S SONS
1897

PREFACE

THE purpose in the present work is to introduce the general as well as the technical Bible student to the essential features of the political, social, and religious life of the Hebrew people. To the candid and thoughtful it is a cause for thanksgiving rather than regret that the earnest scholarship of to-day is carefully sifting the current conclusions concerning the teaching and history contained in the Bible. Although at first the results of this critical study seem only destructive and even alarming, yet a closer examination demonstrates that they are but necessary means to an end. That end is the acquisition of the whole instead of partial truth. The enveloping masses of cloud must be scattered by the sunlight and driving gales, before the outlines of the eternal mountains can be seen in their true proportions. That which dispels human traditions and misconceptions is of inestimable value, because it discloses the real. In reconstructing the facts of Hebrew history in the light of modern biblical research, however, positive rather than negative results command attention. It is sufficient in most cases to ignore the old conceptions, which have been proved incorrect, and to present established conclusions.

Recognizing that some of the questions necessarily treated are still in the state of being answered, I have introduced into the text full biblical references, that the reader may personally investigate the grounds for the deductions. In the same connection special attention is called to the authorities cited in the Appendix, where definite page references are given under each chapter heading. These also indicate in part the debt which I owe to those who have laid the foundations for the new history of the Hebrew people. In the same class may properly be included the many University and University Extension students with whom it has been my privilege to consider this important chapter of human history, and whose valuable suggestions are herein incorporated.

No apology is required for devoting so much attention to the historical sources. The general reader is entirely justified in demanding a view of the foundations as well as of the superstructure of a history so important as that of the Hebrew people. All technical terms, however, are avoided, and only those results presented which are intelligible to students of the English Bible who are familiar with historical and literary methods of study. For the more detailed and technical treatment of each subject the reader is again referred to the Appendix.

The early history of the Israelitish tribes, when viewed in the uncolored light of the oldest records, appears at first quite different from that to which we were introduced by our parents. But reflection soon demonstrates that nothing essential to faith or the Old

Testament revelation has been lost. In reality the difference between the present and the earlier view is chiefly one of language and form of expression. The Hebrews were right in seeing God in everything, and in attributing all that came to them directly to his influence; but they knew no distinction between the natural and the supernatural. Even the idea associated with the word "natural" was yet unborn. They accordingly classified the most ordinary phenomena of life as supernatural. A pestilence or eclipse was regarded as a superlative miracle. The discovery of natural laws has radically changed our conception of history as well as of Nature. God, however, is by no means read out of his universe because we are able to follow and understand the methods whereby he realized his divine purpose through the Hebrew people. Instead, the old Hebrew conception of God in everything is expanded and vindicated.

"And God is seen God
In the star, in the stone, in the flesh, in the soul, and the clod."

True, "Israel was hewn from the rock" by the action of much the same forces within and without which have been employed in all ages by the Highest to accomplish his supreme ends. The winds that blew back the waters of the Red Sea were like other winds. If the testimony of travellers is to be accepted, the phenomenon itself is not without parallel. But its opportuneness was the result of no mere chance. So also, not only at the crises, but throughout Hebrew history, we recognize the hand of God in the wind and storm, in the configuration of the land of Canaan, in the environment of the Israelites, in the events of their national experience, and in the voices of their enlightened prophets, priests, and wise men. Not all at once, but by a long and painful process were the barbarian nomads developed into a nation with a message and mission to humanity. It does not, therefore, at all shake our faith in that message to find that in life and thought the early Hebrews were very like other races in the corresponding stages of their development.

While we have lost nothing in adopting the modern point of view, our new history of the Hebrew people becomes living and real. Its heroes seem at home in their surroundings. They command our admiration, not because they were perfect, but because, laboring under all the limitations of their age, they were struggling, though afar, toward perfection. With a true historical perspective, not a few of the perplexing questions which have caused so many in the past to stumble are easily and satisfactorily answered. In this new light also we are able for the first time to appreciate justly the work and teachings of the Hebrew prophets. The evidence of a progressive development running through Israel's history brings it into closer relations with all history and with the universe, where God's law of progress is dominant. In this simple way we are led to realize that the ancient Hebrews are not creations of the fancy; nor are they dead, but still live, as they firmly believed they would, in the abounding life of humanity. Therefore, we watch with a personal interest the faint glimmers of spiritual light which broke through the darkness of heathenism, and gradually became brighter and brighter until inspired prophets were able to herald in the distance the rising Sun of Righteousness in whose full light we stand to-day.

It is perhaps needless to add that I am fully aware of the difficulties of the task which has been undertaken, and how imperfectly it has been performed. No one who believes that through the life and literature of the Hebrew race the most precious revelation of God is conveyed to man, can maintain for a moment that he or any age has grasped more than a part of the truth therein contained. Therefore, the conclusions which I present are laid before the public with the earnest hope that where they are entirely or partially incorrect they may be speedily disproved by the fuller truth.

C. F. K.

PROVIDENCE, March, 1896.

CONTENTS

PART I

INTRODUCTORY STUDIES

I

THE SCOPE AND IMPORTANCE OF HEBREW HISTORY

SECTIONS 1–3. PAGES 3–6.

II

THE SOURCES OF HEBREW HISTORY

SECTIONS 4–11. PAGES 7–17.

III

THE LAND OF THE HEBREWS

IV

THE ANCIENT TRIBES INHABITING CANAAN

V

THE GENESIS OF THE HEBREW PEOPLE

PART II

THE SETTLEMENT IN CANAAN AND THE PREPARATION FOR THE UNITED KINGDOM.

I

HISTORICAL SOURCES FOR THIS PERIOD

II

SETTLEMENT AND FINAL LOCATION OF THE HEBREW TRIBES

III

HEBREW CHAMPIONS AND WARS OF DELIVERANCE

IV

ORIGIN AND HISTORY OF THE KINGDOM OF GIDEON

SECTIONS 54–56.   PAGES 79–83.

V

THE PHILISTINE YOKE

SECTIONS 57–61.   PAGES 84–88.

VI

SOCIAL AND RELIGIOUS CONDITIONS DURING THE PERIOD OF THE JUDGES

SECTIONS 62–72.   PAGES 89–98.

PART III

THE HISTORY OF THE UNITED KINGDOM

I

HISTORICAL SOURCES

II

STEPS LEADING TO THE ESTABLISHMENT OF THE HEBREW KINGDOM

III

THE DECLINE OF SAUL, AND THE RISE OF DAVID

VII

DAVID'S FOREIGN WARS AND CONQUESTS

SECTIONS 117-120. PAGES 147-150.

VIII

THE ORGANIZATION OF DAVID'S KINGDOM

SECTIONS 121-124. PAGES 151-153.

IX

DAVID'S FAMILY HISTORY

SECTIONS 125-133. PAGES 154-160.

X

THE CHARACTER AND WORK OF DAVID

SECTIONS 134-138. PAGES 161-168.

XI

THE ACCESSION OF SOLOMON

Sections 139–142. Pages 169–175.

Section 139. The question of the succession. 140. Conspiracy of Adonijah and the crowning of Solomon. 141. Execution of the king's enemies. 142. Character and court of the new ruler.

XII

THE FOREIGN AND HOME POLICY OF SOLOMON

Sections 143–153. Pages 176–188.

Section 143. The successful rebellions in Edom and Syria. 144. The strongholds of Israel. 145. Foreign commerce. 146. Alliances. 147. Results of commerce and alliances. 148. Solomon's splendor. 149. The bondage of his subjects. 150. Their discontent. 151. Solomon's wisdom. 152. Solomon as a proverb-maker. 153. The fruits of his folly.

XIII

THE PALACE AND TEMPLE OF SOLOMON

Sections 154–159. Pages 189–195.

Section 154. Solomon's aim in building the Temple. 155. Location of the royal buildings. 156. The palace. 157. The Temple. 158. Its environs. 159. Its architectural design.

XIV

SOCIAL AND RELIGIOUS CONDITIONS UNDER THE UNITED KINGDOM

SECTIONS 160–169. PAGES 196–206.

LIST OF MAPS.

PART I

INTRODUCTORY STUDIES

I

SCOPE AND IMPORTANCE OF THE HISTORY OF THE HEBREW PEOPLE

1. In southwestern Asia, lying between the eastern shores of the Mediterranean Sea and the Arabian desert, is a little territory, to-day called Palestine, but known in antiquity as Canaan. At the time when the civilization of Egypt had already reached its height, when the rich life of Greece was just beginning to unfold, and when the Roman Empire was as yet unborn, there lived among these hills and valleys a Semitic people known in history as the Benê-Israel. By their neighbors they were designated as the Hebrews, " the people from beyond the river." The roots of their history are found in the life of certain nomadic Semitic tribes, who, after dwelling for a few generations in the neighborhood of the Nile Delta, broke away from the enthralling yoke of Egypt, and turned eastward to seek their former home. But their history as a people first assumed definite form when, ceasing from their desert wanderings, they seized the territory east of the Jordan, and began to cross the river in quest of a settled abode. It therefore properly begins with the settlement in Canaan (about 1200 B. C.), and

3

extends down to the fall of Jerusalem in 586 B. C., when the distinct national life of the Hebrews came to an end. The remnant which came back from the captivity at Babylon to rebuild Jerusalem and found a new state were Jews; and with them Jewish history begins.

2. The history of the Hebrew people considers not only the political but also the religious forces and conditions which moulded and characterized their life. It focuses the attention upon a certain nation. Consequently, it is distinguished on the one hand from Old Testament history, which records God's self-revelation and activity among men; and on the other from the contemporary history of the Old Testament, which considers the national life of the peoples who touched and influenced the Hebrews, and who, as a result, are mentioned in the canonical writings. The necessity of keeping these distinctions constantly in mind is obvious; for not only the content but also the aim and method of investigation in each is different. Old Testament history, for example, gives little heed to historical proportion; political and social events are of secondary importance. On the contrary, the revelation of Jehovah, which it treats as its central theme, is regarded as only one of many elements in the history of the Hebrew people. Since the latter is a part of the world history, the same scientific methods which have approved themselves in the study of the history of other nations should be applied here. Though quite distinct in subject and aim, these three related departments of history overlap each other. The textbook of Old Testament history, the Bible, is also the great source of information respecting the Hebrew

people. Hebrew history, however, gathers its material from other sources as well as from the Bible. Old Testament history, on the other hand, does not confine its attention exclusively to any one race. Contemporary history, although in a sense broader than both the preceding, is chiefly valuable for the light which it sheds upon the life of the Hebrew people.

3. Two great currents of thought and influence flow out of the past. United, they determine to a great extent the character of that which is to-day called "civilization." Hellenism contributed the elements of philosophy, art, and political organization, and the canons of scientific thought; but this fair stream, abounding in so much that stimulated human progress, was pitiably destitute in that which is the basis of higher good. This was religion. Rising farther back in human history, there came from the barren hills of Canaan that other current which furnished those absolute essentials to the highest civilization, — religion, ethics, and the elements of the laws which regulate the relations of man to man and to his God. In the history of the Hebrew people, therefore, one may follow the unfolding in the mind of man, under the influence of the Divine, of those great religious ideas which have become the mainspring of humanity's progress, and which have determined the nature of the faith of more than half mankind. For, crystallizing, they became the religion of the Jew; being perverted, they degenerated into Mohammedanism; and, expanding, they developed into Christianity. The Hebrews also first taught man that the supreme goal of life is righteousness. Consequently, they are the great ethical teachers of humanity. Hand

in hand with ethics went its objective expression, —
law. To-day the elements of the Hebrew legislation
have become the bone and marrow of the world's
greatest legal systems. In grappling with the social
problems of their age, the enlightened Hebrew prophets, priests, and wise men deduced social laws which
are as applicable in the present as they were twenty-
five hundred years ago. Therefore, for the student of
religion, law, and social science Hebrew history pos-
sesses a pre-eminence shared with no other. It also
furnishes the historical background without which the
literature and thought of the Old Testament is only
half intelligible. To one who recognizes in that
unique history the unique revelation of God to man,
it is the history of all histories.

THE SOURCES OF HEBREW HISTORY

4. THE historian Von Ranke, when asked how it was that he was able to write history which stood the test of time, replied, "I do not go back *to*, but back *of*, the documents." By this he meant that he did not at once incorporate into his history every monkish tale which came within his reach. Instead, he first determined the age and point of view of each ancient manuscript from which he gleaned his information. Then he was able, by making due allowance for the personal and time equation, to sift out and use the elements of fact which it contained. The rule is equally applicable to all history. Before a lasting structure can be reared, a firm foundation must be laid. In order to do this, all the material which is to go into the foundation must first be tested. Especial care in sifting the sources is demanded in the case of Hebrew history, for the reason that its events are so far removed from the present. Of its many sources, by far the richest is the Old Testament. This is in reality a great library, containing the remnants of a nation's literature. It consists of books and parts of books, coming from many different epochs and authors, who write from different points of view and with different aims. The modern Occidental student often finds it confusing and almost unintelligible, because the material

is not arranged systematically. Classification is therefore the first requisite. A quotation from the mouth
of the enemies of the prophet Jeremiah (Jer. xviii. 18)
suggests a system both fundamental and practical:
" For the law shall not perish from the priest, nor
counsel from the wise, nor the word from the prophet."
It introduces the three great classes of workers who
guided and moulded Hebrew life, and refers to their
characteristic literary products.

5. Superior to their contemporaries in consecration,
intelligence, and earnestness, and enlightened by Jehovah, the Hebrew prophets saw facts and truths unknown to their contemporaries. They were by virtue
of the possession of this deeper knowledge equipped
and commissioned to proclaim to their countrymen, as
his ambassadors, the message of the Highest. A di-
vinely inspired ideal of righteousness and perfection
filled their souls. Their eager endeavor to realize that
ideal in their nation — so unwise in its policy and so
corrupt in its character — made them statesmen, social
reformers, and religious and ethical teachers. By stirring address, by public tablet, and by symbolic action,
they sought to impress the great truths which had been
revealed to them upon their less enlightened contemporaries. In time also they were led to commit their
" word " to writing. Thus it was in divine providence
that the oral prophecies became a part of the Old
Testament.

The literary activity of the prophets, however, did
not cease here. Suggestions of another type of teaching
are found even in the oral prophecies. It is unfortu-
nate that to-day the meaning of the word " prophet "
is so sadly restricted, for it leads to much popular

misconception. According to its derivation the word does not necessarily mean "one who foretells," but merely "one who speaks for another." The Hebrew word simply signifies a speaker. Exodus vii. 1, 2 refers to Aaron as the prophet of Moses, when he acts as the latter's spokesman and representative before the people. As has been well said, the Hebrew prophets were not foretellers but forthtellers. Sometimes their message took the form of a prediction respecting the future; more frequently it consisted of burning addresses on the living political, social, and religious questions of their day. Often the prophet, recognizing that his hearers had failed to grasp the great truths and principles which he was endeavoring to present, would pause and introduce some familiar illustration which would make his meaning patent to the mind of the most obtuse. Ordinarily, he drew his illustrations from the rich storehouse of his nation's remarkable experience. Thus for the moment he would be teaching, not by prophecy of the future nor of the present, but of the past. The last may be defined as the use of past history, narrative, or tradition to impress and illustrate prophetic truth. This lucid and efficient method of teaching was very popular with both people and prophet. Several of the Old Testament books may be classified as purely prophecy of the past. The Jews in their older arrangement of the scriptures, recognizing this fact, designated Joshua, Judges, I. and II. Samuel, and I. and II. Kings as the " Earlier Prophets," to distinguish them from the other prophecies (Isaiah to Malachi inclusive) which they styled the "Later Prophets." To the first class may properly be added the little Book of Ruth (which is parallel to the narratives of the Book of Judges), and parts of the Pentateuch. Similarity in language and literary style, and community of ideas and contents, distinguish these books and parts of books from other portions of the Old Testament, and indicate clearly that they are from prophetic writers. A common aim appears in them all. Historic proportion is quite disregarded. For example, in the Book of Samuel the important battle of Gilboa is treated in a few verses, while the relations between Samuel (the prophet) and Saul occupy several chapters.

This and kindred facts are explained when the aim of the prophetic writer is fully appreciated. For him events in themselves were of little importance, since his purpose was not merely to write a history of his people; instead, it was primarily and simply to teach spiritual truth. To attain this exalted end, he was as ready to employ a late tradition as an early narrative. Often when he found two accounts of the same event he introduced both of them, even though this involved small contradictions and historic inaccuracies. If he had had the data at his command whereby he could determine which of the two was the older and therefore the more authentic record, he probably would not have deemed it worthy of his attention, for it would not have rendered his teaching any more effective with his contemporaries. His historic knowledge also was that of his age; the narratives and traditions which he incorporated in his writings were those with which his contemporaries were familiar. If he was writing of a period antedating his own by centuries, he was wholly dependent upon the testimony of others. The prophetic author of Samuel and Kings makes frequent reference to certain written records which he was able to consult, — as for example the Chronicles of the Kings of Judah and Israel; but for data respecting the earlier epochs, when writing was exceedingly rare, they seem to have been almost entirely dependent upon popular tradition. These ordinarily collected about certain places or customs. When the women in later years went to draw water at the famous well mentioned in Numbers xxi. 16, they sang the song found in the verses which follow this reference. The song preserved the remembrance of the events which took place centuries before about the ancient well. The memories of Deborah clustered about the venerated palm-tree of Deborah (Judges iv. 5), just as those of Abraham were associated with his tamarisk at Beersheba. Certain towns regarded one or another of the patriarchs as their patron saint, and consequently cherished the traditions respecting him. At Bethel, Jacob, and at Hebron, Abraham, were thus immortalized. Frequently it was around some striking monument, which aroused the curiosity of succeeding generations, that the stories gathered. The grave of Rachel recalled the tales respecting Jacob's favorite wife (Gen. xxxv. 20), as did the cave of Machpelah those respecting the patriarchs (Gen. xxiii. 9–20), and Absalom's tomb (II. Sam. xviii. 17) the fate of David's rebellious son. Similar reminders were the heap of stones in the Jordan (Josh. iv. 9), which the author of Joshua declares was still standing when he wrote his history. The heaps in the valley of Achor (Josh. vii. 26) and at Ai (Josh. viii. 29) recalled the conquest of Canaan. About the local shrines, as for example Bethel and Dan, also gathered a mass of traditions.

As the maidens in the east-Jordan land came each year to bewail the tragic death of Jephthah's daughter, they kept alive the memories of the deeds of that ancient chieftain. Sometimes it was merely a popular proverb — as for example, I. Sam. x. 12; xix. 24, "Is Saul among the prophets?" — that. recalled an incident which otherwise might have been forgotten.

From these many sources the prophets gleaned their illustrations and the data wherewith they reconstructed the outlines of their nation's history, which was itself a supreme illustration of the truths concerning Jehovah which they wished to impress. Scientific or historic accuracy they did not claim. One's respect, however, for the Old Testament and the work of the prophets deepens when it is perceived that they were subject to all the limitations of an era when scientific methods of investigation were unknown and the exact historic spirit still unborn. The scientific and historical variations are in themselves proofs of the truth of the divine message which was thus given forth in a form attractive and intelligible to all. At the same time it is obvious that if the modern student is to become acquainted with the real facts of Hebrew history, he must do that for which the prophets had neither the desire nor the equipment, — that is, he must "go back of the documents" and carefully analyze each narrative, asking what was the date and point of view from which it was written.

6. While the prophets were putting their messages in permanent literary form, the second group of Israel's teachers — the priests — was not inactive. Their chief functions during their great literary period were to care for the national sanctuaries and perform the

ceremonial rites; they were the appointed guardians of the ritual. Probably for centuries the sacred laws and customs were transmitted by word of mouth, or only partially committed to writing; but at last there came a time when convenience or existing conditions demanded that they be codified. The origin and history of these laws also became a matter of interest and importance. Therefore the priests were led, like the prophets, to become historians. This fact explains the presence of the parallel histories, which are found interwoven in the Pentateuchal books side by side with those that bear the prophetical stamp. Here again common language, literary style, thought-realm and aim distinguish these historico-legal sections from the historico-prophetical, and proclaim their respective relationship. The priestly records contained in I. and II. Chronicles and their continuation, Ezra and Nehemiah, trace the history of the Temple, law, and priesthood down through the Hebrew into Jewish times. A comparison of this contemporary record with that contained in Samuel and Kings illustrates most vividly the difference between the legal and prophetical literature of the Old Testament. Both in part treat of the same period; but the one focuses the attention on the priests, and notices only the Judean kingdom, where their influence was most potent; while the other almost ignores them, and presents the work of the prophets, dwelling at length upon the events in the northern kingdom, where the prophets were the chief spiritual guides. Manifestly, the historico-legal books cannot be called history, in the ordinary sense of the term; for their primary aim is to teach religious truth, and that of a distinctly ritualistic type. Consequently, the data which they contain respecting the political life of the Hebrew people are only incidental.

7. The third class of Hebrew teachers — the wise men — labored so unobtrusively that their work has been almost unnoticed. They spoke in private to the individual, and not in public to the nation. They were the personified common-sense of their age and race. Ripe in personal experience, keen observers of human nature, enriched by inherited wisdom, they became the advisers of all classes in ancient Israel. Everything that concerned the ordinary man commanded their attention. They were equally ready with practical advice concerning anything, from the purchase of a farm to man's duty to his God. For centuries they taught the masses beside the city gates before they put their "counsel" into written form. The Book of Proverbs is their most characteristic product; it contains the crystallized experience of the enlightened sages. When they came to grapple with the greater problems of life, the Song of Songs, Job, and Ecclesiastes were added to their literature.

8. Two other books, poetical in form, deeply religious in essence, remain, — Psalms and Lamentations. They represent the outpouring of the souls of devout Hebrews of all ages as they came into the presence of Jehovah. They may be designated as the devotional literature of the Old Testament. Praise to the Lord, the source of all blessing, or an earnest cry for deliverance from evil and danger, is the prevailing chord. Prophet, priest, and sage unite with king and peasant in the authorship of this song-book of worshipful humanity.

9. The material in this old library, which is the great

source for Hebrew history, may be classified as follows: Prophetical Literature, — the prophetical portions of the Hexateuch, and Judges, Ruth, Samuel, Kings, Jonah, and the prophecies of the Major and Minor Prophets. Legal Literature, — the priestly portions of the Hexateuch and Chronicles, Ezra, Nehemiah, and Esther. Wisdom Literature, — Proverbs, Song of Songs, Job, and Ecclesiastes. Devotional Literature, — Psalms and Lamentations.

The historical contributions of each of these four classes of literature are of widely different character and value. Since the prophets were the statesmen of Israel and in closest touch with the national movements, their writings contain the most data respecting the political life of the Hebrews; they also present the most definite portraits of the social, religious, and moral conditions. Of all the biblical sources the oral prophecies are the most authentic, since they represent the testimony of eye-witnesses who were the most enlightened men of their times. The legal literature is valuable chiefly for the information which it furnishes respecting the ritualistic side of the Hebrew religion and state. Its priestly histories were written long after the events which they record occurred, and therefore contain little data supplementary to that contained in the prophetical annals. The wisdom literature makes no reference to current political events; it is invaluable, however, as an introduction to the social, domestic, and moral life of the people. Through the devotional literature we are admitted to the sanctuary of the nation's soul, and can study there the play of those deep religious emotions, aspirations, and intuitions which made the Hebrews the spiritual teachers of humanity, and rendered their history unique.

10. Up to the present century, the information respecting the life of the Hebrews was limited almost exclusively to that contained in the Old Testament. Recent discoveries, however, have thrown a flood of light upon that ancient history. The hieroglyphic literature of the Nile valley, now supplemented by the cuneiform tablets coming from the fourteenth century B. C., illuminate pre-Hebrew Canaan, and render it possible to understand the conditions under which the Hebrew nation was born. Throughout their national existence the relations between Egypt and Israel were exceedingly intimate; and, consequently, our knowledge of the life of Egypt enables us to elucidate many difficult questions in the history of her sister state. Palestine itself has as yet furnished little monumental literature. Two or three inscriptions of a few lines only are all; but these are sufficient to indicate that the so-called Phœnician script was in use in Israel during the royal period, and that the language represented in the modern Hebrew Bible was very similar to that spoken by David and Isaiah. In the territory of ancient Phœnicia have been discovered a large collection of inscriptions which are especially valuable to the student of Semitic languages and religions. The most important inscription, coming from the Canaanitish group of nations, is the famous Moabite stone, discovered in 1868 east of the Jordan; it was reared by Mesha, one of the Moabite kings mentioned in the Book of Kings (II. iii. 4). The Phœnician system of writing is employed; the vocabulary and grammatical forms are closely analogous to the Hebrew.

For the study of Hebrew history the inscriptions from Assyria and Chaldea have furnished the most important facts. Although they sometimes modify as well as corroborate, they marvellously supplement the biblical testimony; by their aid it is possible to view Hebrew history from without, and to study the Hebrews in the light in which they were regarded by their contemporaries. Far less reliable, but yet suggestive, are the later traditions which have been preserved in Greek, Hebrew, and Mohammedan writings, or are still current in the mouth of the Arab-speaking peoples. By carefully studying these according to the laws which govern the growth of tradition, it is often possible to extract the kernel of truth which they contain.

11. The spade has turned up not merely inscriptions, but also many a remnant of ancient Oriental civilization. Archæology, therefore, contributes its valuable information respecting the home-life and material surroundings of the Hebrews. The modern customs of the Orient, "which changeth not," are a most fertile source of knowledge respecting the social life of the Israelites. The comparatively new science of historical geography also introduces the student to the background of the historic events, and discloses those natural conditions which were so effective in moulding the life of the Hebrew people. The task of the Hebrew historian is first to analyze this varied material, and then to combine it into a co-ordinated, living whole.

III

THE LAND OF THE HEBREWS

12. THE land of the Hebrews is situated between
31° and 33° 20′ north latitude, and 34° 20′ and 36° east
longitude. It is bounded on the north by Mount
Hermon and the base of the Lebanons; on the east by
the Arabian desert; on the south by the wilderness of
Judah, an extension of the Arabian desert; and on the
west by the coast plains. At certain periods of Hebrew history it included portions of these plains, and
even touched the Great Sea between Joppa and Carmel. This territory, at most one hundred and fifty
miles long and one hundred wide, was only a little
dot on the earth's surface compared with the great
empires about it; but within these narrow boundaries
there was a world in miniature. Six distinct divisions
or zones can be distinguished. Between the Mediterranean and the foot-hills of the central plateau, there
extends a series of coast plains from Beirut to the
River of Egypt; in Phœnicia they are only from two
to six miles in width. South of Tyre the mountains
come down and touch the waters of the sea, forming
the bold promontory called the "Ladder of Tyre."
With this one exception the coast highway extends un-
interruptedly from north to south. Carmel, it is true,
divides the plain of Acre from its southern complement, Sharon; but a narrow strip of land by the sea

at the northern end of the mountain connects them.
South of Carmel, Sharon ever broadens until it merges
into the fertile plain of Philistia, which rolls away
eastward from the sea for twenty or thirty miles until
it breaks against the foot-hills of Judah. Nature
smiles upon these fruitful, well-watered plains; they
are the richest garden and harvest fields of Palestine.
At the same time they are the most exposed to the
attack of an invader from north and south, and least
easily defended.

13. Opposite Joppa, the mountains of the central
range begin to descend more leisurely to the plain.
Southward to the Judean desert, there runs a series of
low foot-hills separated from the central plateau by a
broad, longitudinal valley, which extends from north
to south like a broad, shallow moat. These foot-hills,
widening from five to fifteen miles, were the debatable
ground between Judah and Philistia. They correspond
closely in physical contour, and in the rôle which they
played in history, to the border lands of southern
Scotland.

14. The third and most important zone is the central plateau. Here was the true home of the Hebrews,
who were always a hill-people as distinguished from
the Canaanites of the plain. Opposite Mount Hermon,
the two distinct lines of the Lebanons deploy into the
broken mountains of Galilee. Shut in by these lofty
peaks are found a series of elevated plateaus, well
watered by the streams that come down from the
Lebanons, and capable of supporting in secluded security a large population. Farther to the south, the
central plateau is interrupted by the plain of Esdraelon,
which with its branches extends across from the Medi-

terranean to the Jordan valley; but below the plain
the central range reappears in the mountains of Samaria. This is a region of marked fertility. From the
very mountain-tops springs gush forth, clothing them
with that rich verdure which in the East is always
insured by the presence of water; broad valleys, with
productive grain-fields, extend throughout the land in
every direction. While these give wealth to the inhabitants, they invite the foreign trader and invader.
The transition from the mountains of Samaria to those
of Judah is marked by the most striking changes.
The broad valleys contract, leaving only narrow, rocky
gorges; the green, verdure-covered hills disappear;
billowy waves of grim, gray limestone extend as far as
the eye can reach. Here Mother Earth has little
nourishment for her children. The streams are rushing torrents during the rainy season, and dry, rocky
wadies in the summer; only a half-dozen perennial
fountains are found in all the territory of Judah.
Water, the necessity of all life, is stored up during the
spring in innumerable rock-cut cisterns for the long,
parching summer months. Thirsty, rugged, barren
Judah! one wonders how it ever supported even the
sparsest population. To the south and east the central
plateau gradually descends, becoming barer and more
barren, until it merges into the wilderness of Judah.

15. The fourth zone is the deep chasm of the Jordan, which divides the land of the Hebrews into two
parts. This huge gorge extends like a great canal
from the foot of Mount Hermon to the arm of the
Red Sea. Springing from the roots of the Lebanons,
the Jordan starts on its southern course. The valley
is at this point about five miles wide, and is bordered

on either side by rounded cliffs which rise to the height of two thousand feet. After rushing along for twelve miles, measured in a straight line, the Jordan checks its speed and wanders leisurely through the tropical tangle of reeds and marsh-land known as Lake Huleh; thence the river flows swiftly down between its high banks for twelve and a half miles more, to discharge its waters into blue Galilee. This heart-shaped expanse of water, twelve and a half miles long and six wide, is almost surrounded by steep cliffs, which rise abruptly to the height of between one thousand and fifteen hundred feet. After lingering at this beautiful lake, — which is itself six hundred and eighty-two feet below the Mediterranean, — the Jordan takes its final plunge toward the centre of the earth; with infinite windings, in the midst of a tangle of tropical vegetation, between towering cliffs, it pursues its rapid course until it pours its waters into the Dead Sea. On the last journey it receives many important tributaries. Down over the western banks the Nahr-el-Jalûd, from its source under the brow of Gilboa and the Farah, comes tumbling; from the highlands of Gilead, east of the Sea of Galilee, the Yarmuk issues to contribute a volume of water equal to that of the Jordan itself; still farther south, the Jabbok also mingles its waves. All the zones in Palestine broaden as one goes southward. Even so the valley of the Jordan expands into the once fertile plain of Jericho, which is fourteen miles in width above the Dead Sea. This sea of death — lying twelve hundred feet below the surface of the ocean, with its bitter, heavy waters, its barren shores which tell the story of an ancient inland sea, and its stupendous system of evaporation, in which six million tons of water rise to heaven each day — is a fitting conclusion to this marvellous series of Nature's wonders.

16. Across the Jordan valley, the bold headlands of Gilead and Moab tower to the height of from two to four thousand feet. Numerous streams furrow their rounded sides, irrigating the elevated plateaus. Heavy dews throughout the year refresh the plains and cover them with a temperate vegetation. Gradually these grass-covered rolling fields become barer and more level, until they merge into the Arabian desert on the east. It is the land both of the agriculturist and of the shepherd. Its rich fields attract the desert nomads, and no natural boundaries appear to keep them out. Hence it was the scene of those important transitions whereby the wandering sons of the desert were gradually transformed into settled agricultural peoples.

17. The sixth and last zone, although not parallel with the others, is in a sense the most important of them all. It is the great plain of Esdraelon, or Jezreel, which cuts across the central plateau, dividing the north from the south. The plain itself is in the form of a triangle, — with one angle under the shadow of Mount Carmel, another at Jenîn in the southeast, and the third at Shunem, under Little Hermon. Fourteen miles straight away can be measured from Jenîn to the foot of the Nazareth hills. But from the central triangle stretches of plain run out in every direction into the territory about. On the west, it joins the coast plain of Acre; to the north, another plain runs up past Mount Tabor into central Galilee; on the east, another extends past Gilboa and Bethshean to the

Jordan and the plateau of Gilead beyond; to the south, it opens into a series of broad plains which intersect Samaria; along the southeastern end of Mount Carmel, it connects by means of a wide valley with the rolling fields of Sharon.

It is manifest why Esdraelon was the great battle-field of Hebrew history. Across its wide expanse ran the highways of the Oriental world, even as does to-day the railroad from Haifa to Damascus. It was the key to Palestine; and Palestine was the key to the East. All the great world-conquerors, from Thotmes III. to Napoleon, recognized this fact. Aside from its importance as a commanding position, it was a desirable possession. Ploughing its way serpent-like across the plain flows the Kishon, little more than a muddy ditch, but sufficient for perfect irrigation. Fountains on every side also contribute their waters. Not even a roll disturbs its level bosom. The soil is fertile and easy to till. It was the great harvest-field of northern Israel, in which many who did not sow were eager to reap.

18. In the land of Palestine the most marvellous contrasts confront one within the limits of a few miles. The coast plains and Esdraelon, with their rich harvest-fields, are the true home of the agriculturist. Judah, on the other hand, supports only a few flocks and rock-encircled vineyards among its barren hills. A half-day's journey brings the traveller from the winter snows of Jerusalem to the tropical luxuriance of the Jordan valley, and another day of travel will introduce him to the barren wastes of the Arabian desert. From certain vantage-points one may see the columns of vapor rising from that great caldron, the Dead

Sea, and with almost the same glance behold the
snowy heights of Mount Hermon. The temperate,
tropical, and frigid zones are each represented in Palestine. On the coast plains the mean temperature is
70°, varying from 50° to 85°; the average temperature
in Jerusalem is 62°, while in the Jordan valley the
extremes are 77° and 118°; up on the highlands of
Gilead frost often appears on the ground in the morning, while by midday the temperature stands at 80°.
Corresponding to these differences in climate are the
contrasts in flora and fauna. The firs overshadow the
palms. Here the wolf of the north contends with the
leopard of the south over the carcass of the gazelle of
the temperate zone. It is evident why the Bible is a
book intelligible to peoples living in all climes, since
that land which is its background is an epitome of
the entire world.

19. Palestine itself is the first chapter in God's
great volume of revelation inscribed upon the history
of the Hebrew people. It is therefore with reverence
that one reads this introductory chapter written upon
the bosom of the earth; for the location of the land
of the Hebrews determined very largely the rôle which
they were to play in the world's history. The first
general characteristic of that land which suggests
itself is its seclusion. Not only is it a unit complete
in itself, but it is also shut in from the rest of the
world. On the north are the frowning peaks of the
Lebanons; on the east and south are the waves of
the Arabian desert; and on the west is the unbroken
line of the Mediterranean, which forbade rather than
invited commerce. During most of their history the
Hebrews were surrounded by a circle of hostile nations,

which like a ring of fire confined them to themselves.
The rivers of Palestine — the ordinary highways along
which a people come into contact with their neighbors — are, with the exception of the Jordan, only
creeks. The current of this river is far too rapid for
navigation, and loses itself in the stagnant waters of
the Dead Sea. Thus through Nature and man the
Father of all commanded the Hebrews to remain at
home, and furthermore encouraged them in this by pro-
viding all the varied products that could reasonably be
demanded, and still not enough to make them eager to
seek a foreign market.

Paradoxical as it may sound, Palestine is secluded
and yet centrally located. On the southeast were
the dark-skinned dwellers on the Nile, who had long
led the van of civilization; on the northwest, bound
to them by common blood and speech, were the sea-
traders of the ancient world, the Phœnicians; to the
northeast were located the land-traders, the Syrians;
while beyond were the powerful empires of the Tigris
and Euphrates. Canaan was the bridge uniting the
two continents of Asia and Africa; on every side
and through her ran the great highways of the
nations. On the south lay the trans-desert road
from Egypt, through Petra and Duma to the Per-
sian Gulf, and on the east the caravan route, as
to-day, from Damascus to the Red Sea and Arabia;
up along the coast plains went the caravans from
Egypt to Phœnicia and the north; another branch of
this great coast road, cutting across the southeastern
end of Mount Carmel and the plain of Esdraelon,
reached Damascus and Assyria and Babylonia beyond.
In their earlier days the Hebrews enjoyed that seclu-

sion which was so necessary for the development of
their national and religious life. When this had been
realized, they were again thrown, by virtue of their
location, into the tempestuous stream of that ancient
world, to learn new lessons in their struggle for existence, and in turn to impart their message to humanity.
Thus the broader outlines of Hebrew history were
marked out long before the Israelites crossed the
Jordan.

IV

20. Situated midway between two continents, Palestine was subject even in the very earliest times to invasion from many sides. Naturally the coast plains were the first to be seized. Later waves of invasion occupied the inland plains, and last of all the rocky mountainous regions. From the Babylonian inscriptions it appears that this process began before the thirtieth century B. C. During this earlier period Babylonian influence was paramount, as is indicated by the character of the civilization and the wide acquaintance with the Babylonian system of writing. Seemingly incapable of a close union, the petty peoples settled in Canaan fell in turn an easy prey to each foreign invader. When the Babylonian power waned, the Egyptian Pharaohs found Palestine a most inviting field for predatory incursions. These became most common in the sixteenth century B. C. Thotmes III. and his successors repeatedly invaded this territory, and carried their arms even to the Euphrates. In the capital towns they placed governors to collect tribute. Thus the Pharaohs established a loose suzerainty over Palestine, which continued down to the twelfth century B. C. The Hittites — a powerful people from the north, probably of non-Semitic origin — for a time successfully contested the rule of this land with the

27

Egyptians; but by the twelfth century B. C. their power was also waning, and they were being supplanted or assimilated by the Aramean peoples from the neighborhood of the Euphrates. The local tribes of Palestine, freed from the thraldom of the foreign invader, were at liberty to crystallize in the manner suggested by their diversified origin, location, and religious peculiarities. Everywhere, and especially among the settled agricultural nations of the plains, were to be found the remnants of those repeated waves of Babylonian and Egyptian civilization which had already for more than ten centuries swept over this much-contested territory.

21. The residuum from these many inundations of foreign immigration and invasion was a mixed and varied population. The plains of western Palestine were occupied by Canaanitish tribes, probably of Semitic origin. Kindred peoples, inhabiting the highlands on the east of the Jordan, are styled by the biblical writers the Amorites. The latter term, however, was not restricted in its application to the east-Jordan tribes, but is frequently used in the Old Testament interchangeably with the general appellation, "Canaanites." These ancient peoples lived in strong walled cities. Each town with its adjacent fields was a little independent kingdom, ruled over by its own chieftain. Agriculture was the principal means of subsistence; foreign trade brought to them the products of the outside world. War between these petty principalities was very common; they united only under the pressure of an impending danger from without. Their religion was the worship of the male and female divinities, Baal and Ashtoreth; it was accompanied

by the most degrading and licentious rites, which tended completely to undermine the social and moral integrity of its devotees. Among the rocky hills of central Palestine, in the less desirable territory, were found ruder shepherd clans, who are designated on the Egyptian monuments as the "Shashu." Possibly they correspond to the biblical Perizzites, the peasants, as contrasted with the Canaanitish villagers, the Hivites. The Phœnicians represented an earlier stratum of immigration, which found a resting-place in the rich coast plains lying along the shores of the Mediterranean. By language, religion, and probably in origin they were closely related to the later immigrants, the Canaanites on the central plains. Their territory was very fruitful, but limited. Restricted on the east by the mountainous headlands, they were led at a very early date to launch out upon the sea. As a result, they became a progressive, opulent race of traders, bearing from nation to nation the products and civilization of that ancient world. They were the connecting link between the secluded tribes of Canaan and the peoples dwelling along the shores of the western sea.

22. In southwestern Palestine, between the western headlands of Judah and the Mediterranean, and bounded by the desert on the south and extending as far as Joppa on the north, is a fertile stretch of rolling plain capable of supporting a large agricultural population. This territory was seized by a hardy, warlike people, who were known as the Philistines, — "wanderers." The nature of their origin is still an unsolved question. They are repeatedly referred to in the Bible as "the people from Caphtor." Captor has been vari-

ously identified. The Egyptian delta scarcely fulfils
the conditions. Most probably it was the island of
Crete. The Egyptian monuments contain significant
references to a sea-people, who are represented as coming southward by boat and wagon. They invaded
Egypt in vast numbers about the time when the Hebrews must have been entering Canaan. They were
repulsed with great slaughter, and forced to turn back
northward along the coast of the Mediterranean to seek
a home in Palestine. The date and details of this invasion are quite in keeping with what is known of the
Philistines from other sources. The territory of these
"wanderers" was divided among their five chief cities,
— Gaza, Askelon, Ashdod, Gath, and Ekron. Each
city was strongly fortified with high, encircling walls,
and was ruled over by its own king. In times of peace
each seems to have acted independently of the others ;
but in their contests with foreign foes they entered
into close and effective union.

23. To the northeast beyond Mount Hermon, and
extending north and east even across the Euphrates,
were the Aramean peoples, who had succeeded in absorbing the territory of the Hittites about the time that
the Hebrews sought a home in Palestine. The Southern Arameans (better known in the English transla-
tions of the Bible as the Syrians) crystallized into a
powerful kingdom, with Damascus as its centre. Agriculture was their chief means of subsistence. By virtue of their intermediate position they became traders,
corresponding on the land to the Phœnicians on the
sea. Their language was a dialect of the Semitic
family. Their national divinities and religious forms
were analogous to those of the Canaanites. This

outer circle of Semitic peoples included the Midianites, Ishmaelites, and Amalekites, whose home was the great Arabian desert, which pressed Palestine on two sides. Up and down its arid wastes they wandered, often making incursions into the territory of their kinsmen who had abandoned the wild, lawless life of the desert for settled homes.

24. Occupying the southern, eastern, and later the central portion of Palestine was another group, including the Moabites, Ammonites, Edomites, and Hebrews. Their traditions traced their origin back to the valley of the Euphrates, and suggested close kinship with the Arameans of the north. Their relationship to one another is attested by community in language and customs, as well as by the biblical record. When they emerge into prominence in history, they are desert tribes, gradually passing over to the agricultural stage. At the period when Hebrew history begins, the Moabites are the most advanced in this transition. Their territory, the uplands to the east of the Dead Sea, was most conducive to this process, for it contained many broad, well-watered fields which invite the ploughman. As a result, the Moabites had large cities, and at an early period became a settled people. Their language, as the Moabite stone attests, was a dialect of Canaan, clearly intelligible to their Hebrew kinsmen across the Dead Sea. They worshipped one tribal deity, whom they called "Chemosh."

To the south of Moab and the Dead Sea, among the barren, rocky cliffs of Mount Seir, which extends southward through the Arabian desert to the arm of the Red Sea, lived the Edomites. Agriculture was possible only along the narrow margins of the deep

wadies; except in a few places the land scarcely furnished sustenance for their flocks. The caravans
which were constantly passing through their territory
brought support to these fierce robbers, who were never
loath to collect their toll. Their mode of life made
them the outlaws of the old Semitic world.

North of Moab, and still farther out on the borders
of the desert, lay the territory of the Ammonites.
The Amorites, and later the Hebrews, possessed the
more desirable land immediately adjacent to the Jordan.
Consequently, the Ammonites were chiefly dependent
upon their flocks for subsistence, and because of the
character of their territory never completely passed
over to agricultural life. They possessed one or two
large cities which gave permanence to their place of
abode; but as a people they stood midway between
the wandering Arab tribes and the settled agricultural
nations of central Palestine. Their language, as the
proper names in the Old Testament indicate, was
(like the Moabite and Edomite) closely related to that
of the Hebrews. Milcom was their one tribal god, to
whom they stood in much the same relations as did the
Hebrews in their early history to Jehovah.

The fourth in this related group of nations was
the Benê-Israel, whose life is the object of the present
study.

THE GENESIS OF THE HEBREW PEOPLE

25. INASMUCH as the present work aims to give a positive picture of the life of the Hebrew nation, it would be aside from the purpose in view to enter upon a detailed investigation of the structure, authorship, and date of the books which contain the records of the pre-national life of the Israelites. Indeed, such an investigation is necessarily hypothetical and unsatisfactory without a previous knowledge of the facts of Hebrew history, which alone furnish a definite starting-point and basis for comparison. No one, however, can unprejudicedly and inductively study the opening books of the Old Testament and fail to recognize therein parallel strands of priestly and prophetical narrative (sects. 5, 6). Sometimes the point of view is Northern Israelitish and sometimes Judean. Not only does the language of different sections suggest that they came from different epochs in the life of the Hebrews, but the thought reflects the different stages through which that people were led to a higher moral and religious consciousness. In the light of these and kindred facts, the conviction grows that the first five books of the Old Testament, like Proverbs (sect. 152), or the distinctly historico-prophetical books (sects. 32–38, 73–84), did not come from one but many prophets and priests, writing at many different periods, but all in the spirit of the

3   33

great prophet-judge with whose name these books are associated. Many of the historical narratives which they contain were evidently not written until centuries after the events which they record had transpired; and there predominates in them all either the prophetical or priestly purpose, which, as has been shown, is by no means identical with the historical (sect. 5). Consequently, it is clear that these books must be carefully analyzed before the historical data which they contain can be intelligently used. In certain general outlines the narratives agree, and are corroborated by the information which comes from the extra-biblical sources. These general conclusions give the student an intelligent conception of the essential facts and forces which characterize the early period when the Hebrew nation was in the making.

26. Wherever the cradle of the race may have been, the united testimony of language, history, and racial characteristics points to northern Arabia as the centre from which the Semitic peoples went forth to the conquest of their respective possessions. The roving tendencies of nomads impelled some at a prehistoric period to gravitate toward the fertile lands adjacent to the Nile; these, fusing with African races, produced the ancient Egyptians. Other bands of emigrants from the home of the race took possession of the productive fields of southern Arabia, and in time streamed across the Red Sea to Africa. This branch, including the nomads who continued to range up and down the great Arabian desert, are known as the Southern Semites. It includes the Arabs, Sabeans, and Ethiopians. Other nomadic tribes, seizing at a very early date the rich territory which lies to the east of the desert and is wa-

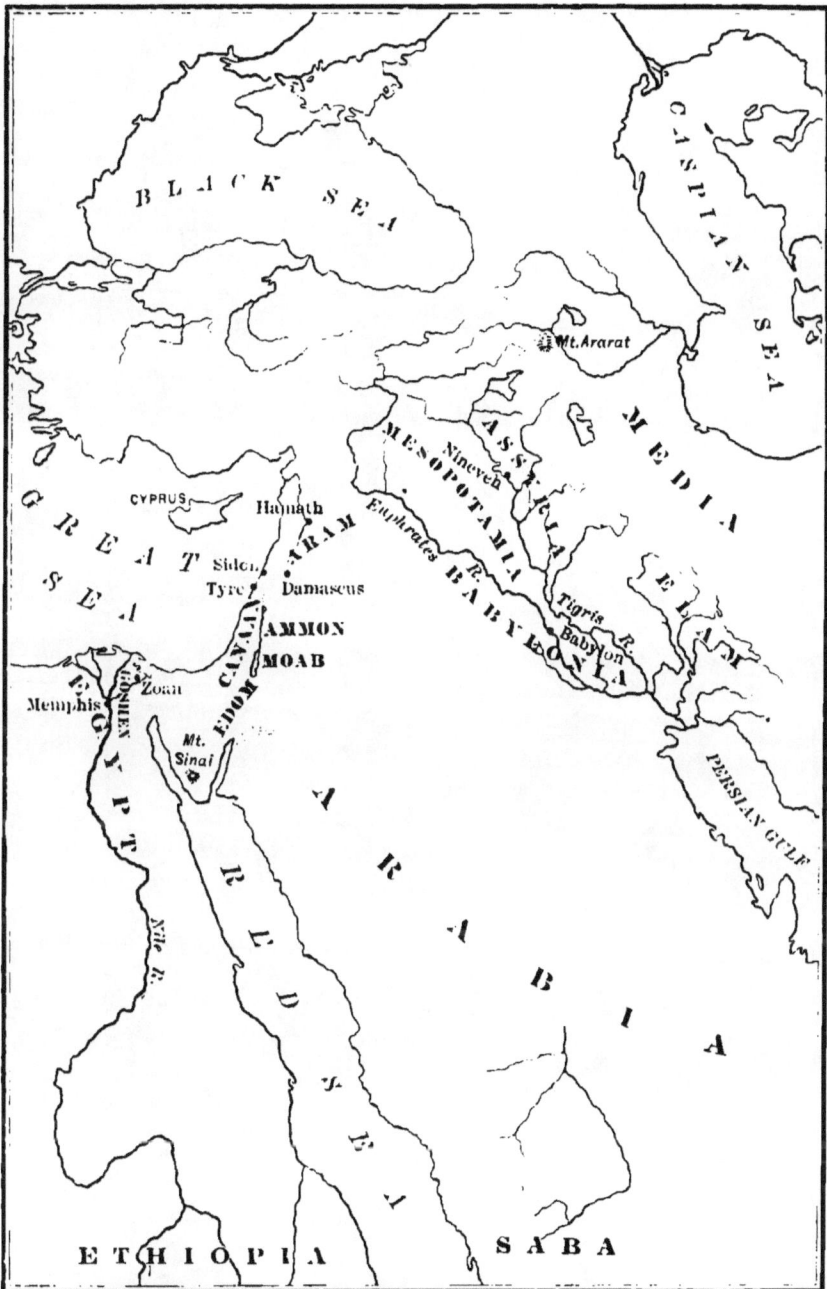

THE ANCIENT SEMITIC WORLD.

tered by the Euphrates and Tigris, founded the powerful empire of ancient Babylonia, which in succeeding
centuries came in turn under the sway of the Assyrians
and Chaldeans.   When the land between the great
rivers became crowded, repeated waves of immigration
surged westward around the northern borders of the
Arabian desert to the attractive agricultural land lying
along the eastern shores of the Mediterranean.   The
first immigrants into Palestine occupied the coast and
inland plains, and became the ancestors of the Canaanites and Phœnicians, who constituted the second group
of the Northern Semites (sect. 21).   The Semites who
settled between the upper waters of the Tigris and Euphrates, and subsequently spread toward the west until
they became masters of the intervening territory even
to the Lebanons (sect. 23), are known in history as the
Arameans, and may be designated as the Aramean
group.

These movements continued during many centuries.
The great centres of Semitic civilization were constantly receiving infusions of new blood from the
desert.   On the other hand, as the valley of the Tigris
and Euphrates became more crowded, bands of emigrants were constantly moving westward in quest of
homes in the less densely settled territory of Palestine.
As the larger groups of the Semitic peoples gradually
crystallized into nations, distinct dialects arose; yet
the points of linguistic likeness which were retained
sufficed to facilitate this interchange of populations.
Consequently, there are good external reasons for
accepting as historical the Hebrew traditions which
represent the ancestors of the Hebrews — and of their
kinsmen the Ammonites, Moabites, and Edomites — as

coming originally from the valley of the Euphrates.
When they entered Palestine they found the more
desirable lands already occupied, and therefore were
obliged to content themselves with what remained. In
time, some of these later immigrants found permanent
homes on the southeastern borders of Palestine; the
others continued to pasture their flocks among the barren uplands of central and southern Canaan. Being
nomads, there was little to hold them in one settled
place of abode. At length, impelled by the same needs
and instincts which since the beginning of history have
led nomadic Semitic tribes to invade the attractive territory along the Nile, they migrated southward and occupied the pasture lands of Goshen located immediately
east of the Nile delta. Although they remained in their
new home for generations, they clung to their language,
customs, and religion with all the tenacity of desert
nomads; they seem also to have kept in touch with
their kinsmen who remained in the wilderness to the
east. As time went on, under the influence of their
more favorable environment, their numbers increased,
until the Pharaohs of Egypt began to regard them as a
menace to the stability of their throne. Forced labor
was consequently imposed upon them. To freedom-
loving nomads such bondage was peculiarly irksome.
But the power of the Egyptians was great, and the
shepherds were unorganized. To flee, which was their
first impulse, was impossible. At last, when their spirit
was all but completely broken, a leader and deliverer
arose in their midst.

27. On the plains of Midian, where he had spent the
days of his opening manhood, Moses had drunk in at
the fountain source the spirit of freedom and the purer

.concepts of Jehovah, the God of his race. There also the Almighty spoke to him, kindling his soul with a new light. Returning with these ideas, he was able to awaken his people to action. In the name of Jehovah, their God and Deliverer, he rallied them. Grievous plagues afflicted the Egyptians, rendering them for the time incapable of checking the shepherds in their sudden flight; with flocks and families, therefore, they set out under the leadership of Moses for Sinai, the abode of their God, and for their former home in southern Canaan. But circumstances led them to turn toward the south, where, beside the arm of the Red Sea, they were overtaken by the Egyptian army sent in pursuit. Their cause seemed hopeless, since they could do little to defend themselves against their well-armed foes. In this crisis a strong east wind arose, which blew all night, driving back the shallow waters so that it was possible for them to pass over (Ex. xiv. 21) and thus escape, while the Egyptians following them perished. In this natural phenomenon — so remarkable, so opportune — the Hebrews ever recognized the delivering hand of their God. It strengthened their wavering faith as nothing else could have done, and by vindicating the assurances of Moses firmly established his authority.

Proceeding eastward from the Red Sea, the march of the Israelites was checked by a powerful desert tribe, the Amalekites. These foes, however, were defeated in battle; and at length the great leader conducted the fugitives safely to the mount of God, which in the Northern Israelitish narrative is called Horeb; in the Judean and priestly records it is known by the more familiar name of Sinai. Here a covenant was estab-

lished, binding the different clans together, and in turn
reuniting them by the closest bonds to their God, Jehovah.   Thence they passed on to Kadesh, a desert station
on the southern limits of Judah.   The more fertile
fields of southern Palestine attracted them, but their
courage failed when they learned the strength of the
inhabitants; consequently, they were obliged to content themselves with the scanty support furnished by
the wilderness.   At Kadesh their sanctuary was located,
and a rude tribunal was established under the direction
of Moses.   Reverting to the habits of their earlier days,
they ranged with their flocks up and down the Arabian
desert, sharing with their kinsmen, the Midianites and
Kenites, the fortunes of a Bedouin people.   The chronological data respecting this early period are exceedingly indefinite, and present variations which it is
difficult to reconcile.   According to the biblical accounts, they remained in the desert for a generation
(forty years).   It was a time of rich religious educa-
tion, for in these barren wastes the shepherds from the
Nile delta appear to have completely rejected any religious concepts which they may have received in Egypt
and to have returned to the purer faith of the desert.
While their religious beliefs were deepening and crystallizing, a feeling of unity was growing among the
tribes, which prepared them for combined action and
constituted the germ of a nation.   A sturdy race,
hardy and brave, was being developed in this most
valuable though severe training-school in which the
Israelites, in accordance with the divine purpose, had
been placed.

    28. At last an opportunity arose to gain possession
of the much-coveted agricultural land which lay on the

borders of the desert. It came, not from the south, but from that territory east of the Jordan which was least defended by natural barriers, and where the transition from barren sand to fruitful pasture and agricultural land was most gradual and natural. The occasion was a protracted war between the Amorites and the kinsmen of the Hebrews, the Moabites and the Ammonites. The former, under their king Sihon, had at some earlier period robbed the Ammonites of their western territory and driven the Moabites to the south of the Arnon. On the scene of their conquests they had built up a strong kingdom, with its capital at Heshbon opposite Jericho. Against this formidable power the Hebrews took the field. They were primarily seeking a home for themselves, but in so doing they were espousing the common interests of the Moabites and Ammonites, whose independence was threatened by the alien kingdom. If not materially assisted by their kinsmen, it is reasonable to believe that they had their sympathy in this undertaking, although the biblical account records only the envy and opposition of the Moabites. The Israelites were successful, and thereby gained a temporary home on the edge of Canaan and in the midst of peoples related to them by blood. The effect of their conquest was far-reaching, for the new land which became their own was adapted to agriculture as well as grazing. At this time began that all-important transition from the nomadic to the agricultural stage, which was destined to alter the very character and faith of " the people from beyond the river."

29. Results point to corresponding causes. If all the Pentateuchal books had been lost, it would still

be necessary to postulate a personality like that of Moses to explain the character of the Israelites as they figure in later history.   The Song of Deborah, which is by all recognized as one of the very oldest pieces of literature in the Old Testament, graphically portrays the disorganized condition of the Hebrews.   Gradually they had been subdued by the Canaanites.   All seemed hopeless, unless something could be found to bind them together and inspire them to fight for freedom.   The sense of kinship was no bond, since already their blood had been mingled with that of the native inhabitants. A common faith in Jehovah was the sufficient and only uniting and impelling force.   Jehovah's prophetess, Deborah, sent out the call to arms.   In the name of the God of Sinai it was issued.   The tribes rallied to the aid of Jehovah, and his curse rested upon those who failed to respond.   From Jehovah came the victory which in Hebrew is always called "deliverance." Almost every verse of that stirring old national song proclaims that the tribes who together styled themselves Israel ("El fights," or "does battle") were the people of Jehovah, and regarded him as their present Leader, Deliverer, and Counsellor.   The faith of a nation is not the growth of a moment nor even of a generation; nor do mere circumstances beget a spiritual religion.   Ordinarily a knowledge of the character and purpose of the Divine is imparted to men through human personality.   In this way the other great religions of the world have arisen, and the Hebrew religion constituted no exception to the rule.

30. Moses is commonly called "the great law-giver of Israel."   This seems to have been the least of his functions.   Primarily, he was a prophet.   Hosea, re-

cognizing this fact, declares, "By a prophet Jehovah brought Israel out of Egypt." It is difficult to determine just what religious ideas Moses inherited from his race. The Old Testament traditions point to a pre-Mosaic conception of Jehovah. Moses could hardly have rallied his kinsmen in Goshen in the name of a God hitherto unknown to them. Union with the tribes of the desert appears to have been easy and natural; but this would have been utterly impossible under the conditions of society existing at that time unless there was among them a close agreement in religion. Ordinarily, the religion of the Israelites is contrasted with the grossly immoral Canaanitish cult with which they were later thrown into contact; but since the Hebrews came from the desert, the genesis of their faith was entirely different. As our knowledge of the religion of the primitive Arabs increases, striking points of similarity with that of the ancient Israelites are constantly disclosed. It is deeply significant that the same terms were employed in each for " worship," "sanctuary," "feast," "jubilee," "offering," "sacrifice," and "seer." In antiquity among the Semites of the desert the gross sex-dualism seems to have been unknown. The arid wastes encouraged simplicity and austerity in religion as well as life; their migratory habits delivered them from the temptation of believing in a multitude of local deities. The god or gods must accompany the tribes if they are to be of any assistance. Sometimes he is conceived of as dwelling on some commanding peak, and coming from thence to succor his suppliants; but ordinarily place is regarded as unimportant to the god as to his wandering worshippers. The tribe was a close corpora-

tion constituting a perfect social unit. The interest of
each individual was synonymous with that of the tribe.
If it was strong, each member prospered in security;
if its interests demanded the life of one of its number,
that life was unhesitatingly given. The whole tribe in
turn was pledged to defend its members.

This feeling of absolute tribal unity and dependence
inevitably aroused a longing for the aid of some supernatural being, — a deity who would give especial heed
to the interests of the community. This one god, then,
became the sole object of the worship of a tribe. His
interests were their interests, and theirs his. Since he
was not originally a member of the clan, he was made
one in the same manner as aliens from another tribe;
namely, by the covenant. Between man and man this
meant at first an interchange of each other's blood,
attended by suitable rites. In time animal blood, wine,
or food was substituted. Since the god was not present in person, the rite was necessarily modified, but the
content was the same. By the covenant he became a
part of the tribe. From time to time this covenant
was renewed. In a sense, each offering to the divinity
was a symbol of union and communion. This type of
tribal organization gave a strong impetus to the worship of one god, and doubtless explains what has been
often styled the Semitic tendency to monotheism.
When a powerful tribe absorbed aliens or other tribes,
the god of the first tribe was necessarily accepted as the
god of all; and thus a tribal deity was exalted to
the position of a national god. Probably this was the
origin of the monolatry which existed among the Edomites, Moabites, and Ammonites who had passed over
from the desert to a settled abode at some period

precedent to the appearance of the Hebrews in Canaan.
The relations of each of these nations to its god were
most intimate. The Moabites for instance, as the
Moabite stone demonstrates, called themselves "the
people of Chemosh," their god. In the name of Chemosh they made war. When he was angry with his
people, he sent defeat and captivity; when victory
came, it was from Chemosh, and to him were dedicated
the fruits of success. He was worshipped with sacrifice and offerings in much the same way as the Hebrews worshipped Jehovah.

These familiar facts suggest the nature of the religious concepts and customs which were the heritage of
Moses from the Semitic past. Like the prophets who
succeeded him, he built upon the revelation already
vouchsafed. The sad condition of his brethren in
Goshen awakened his patriotism as well as his sympathy. The crisis demanded a prophet who could stir
men. Appealing to their religious memories and instincts, which had been rendered dormant in the lotus-
land of Egypt, and to their love of freedom which is
such a passion with nomads, he was able to arouse
them. As they turned their faces toward their old
homes, they were little more than a disorganized body
of fugitives; but a Power higher than Moses was
working with him. The remarkable circumstances
of the exodus made an indelible impression upon the
Israelites. Jehovah, their God, had revealed himself as
a God able and ready to succor his people. These acts
of deliverance, which clearly indicated the attitude of
Jehovah to his people, furnished a fitting introduction
to the covenant at Sinai. There, at the mount which
was then, and even down to the days of Elijah continued

to be, regarded as the especial abode of Jehovah, the bond was established which made Israel Jehovah's peculiar people; and Jehovah, who perhaps before had been but the God of a tribe, became Israel's Leader, Counsellor, Defender, and Deliverer. Naturally and rightly, Moses was received by the people as Jehovah's representative. His words were Jehovah's message to them. As he led them in their wilderness wandering, they felt themselves under the direct guidance of their God; he attended to the simple ritual of the desert sanctuary at Kadesh; to him, as the representative of Jehovah, were referred the more difficult cases of dispute which arose; his decisions had all the weight of Jehovah's authority. In this way he laid down by practical illustration the principles of that civil and religious law which bears his name. As these cases multiplied, he was led to constitute a rude patriarchal tribunal composed of the elders of the tribes (Ex. xviii.). In this simple organization is found the germ of the Hebrew judicial and executive system.

31. Thus Moses was the man who under divine direction "hewed Israel from the rock." Subsequent prophets and circumstances chiselled the rough bowlder into symmetrical form, but the glory of the creative act is rightly attributed to the first great Hebrew prophet. As a leader, he not only created a nation, but guided them through infinite vicissitudes to a land where they might have a settled abode and develop into a stable power; in so doing, he left upon his race the imprint of his own mighty personality. As a judge, he set in motion forces which ultimately led to the incorporation of the principles of right in objective laws. As a priest, he first gave definite form to the

worship of Jehovah. As a prophet, he gathered together all that was best in the faith of his age and race, and, fusing them, gave to his people a living religion. Under his enlightened guidance Israel became truly and forever the people of Jehovah. Through him the Divine revealed himself to Israel as their Deliverer, Leader, and Counsellor, — not afar off, but present; a God powerful and willing to succor his people, and therefore one to be trusted and loved as well as feared. As the acorn contains the sturdy oak in embryo, so the revelation through Moses was the germ which developed into the message of Israel to humanity.

PART II

THE SETTLEMENT IN CANAAN, AND THE PREPARATION FOR THE UNITED KINGDOM

I

32. THE chief source of information respecting the first period of Hebrew history is the Book of Judges. An examination of this old writing soon discloses the fact that it was not cast in its present form primarily for the purpose of recording history, but rather to teach and illustrate spiritual truth. This explains why the early Hebrews, recognizing its dominant religious aim, classified it under the head of prophetical literature (cf. sect. 9). The lesson which its prophetical author was endeavoring to impress by the illustrations which he drew from the lore of his nation is presented in the constantly occurring formula, "And the children of Israel did that which was evil in the sight of Jehovah ; . . . and the anger of Jehovah was kindled against Israel, and he sold them into the hands of ——, and they served —— years ; . . . and the children of Israel cried unto Jehovah, and he raised up unto them a savior, . . . and the land had rest —— years." The exploits of each of the greater judges are introduced in this manner. These formulas, therefore, are the framework into which the earlier narratives that constitute the body of the book are fitted. Naturally the portions of chief importance to the student of Hebrew history are the ancient records

4   49

thus preserved. Moreover, their value is greatly en-
hanced because the prophetic writers have not recast,
but instead, in most cases, have transcribed them verbatim from the earlier sources, adding only such introductory matter as seemed to be necessary for their
purpose. Although these extracts are broken and
incomplete, and sometimes fit awkwardly into their
stereotyped setting, they give true glimpses into the
conditions which existed in that early period. Literary style and contents testify to their antiquity, and
suggest that they were committed to writing not long
after the events, which they record, occurred. Consequently, although not nearly so full of details, they
are a far richer field from which to glean historic facts
than the Book of Joshua, which abounds in the language and ideas of a later age. In the latter book,
for example, conquests and conditions which were not
completely realized until the reigns of David and Solomon are compressed into a space of about seven years.
So great is the foreshortening that in a sense the Book
of Joshua, in its present form, may properly be regarded as an epitome of the history of the united Hebrew kingdom. Just how far in individual cases it
presents the testimony of authentic tradition, or the
concepts of a later age respecting this early period, is
one of the most difficult questions which confront the
historian. It is one which can be answered only after
a careful study of its language and ideas, in connection with the early portions of Judges and in the light
of subsequent conditions.

33. The Book of Judges consists of (1) an introduction, i. 1–ii. 5; (2) the history of the Judges, ii. 6–xvi.
31; and (3) an appendix, xvii.–xxi. The opening words

of the introduction, " And it came to pass after the
death of Joshua," were evidently added by some later
editor of the book for the purpose of connecting it as a
sequel to the Book of Joshua, after which it is placed.
This is somewhat misleading, since the first chapter of
Judges treats of the same events and periods as the
Book of Joshua. Chapter ii. also recounts events
which occurred while Joshua was living, and tells of
his death and burial. The material preserved in the
introduction (Judges i. 1^b–ii. 5) was evidently taken
from ancient tribal records, and sheds an almost contemporary light upon the settlement in Canaan. More
than half the section is devoted to recounting the
failures of the Hebrews to dispossess the Canaanites,
thus presenting a picture in perfect harmony with subsequent conditions. It is also interesting to note that
the testimony of this section is corroborated by a series
of passages scattered through the Book of Joshua,
which are loosely connected with the context and
which represent the older strata. In such passages
as Judges i. 20^b, 10^b–15, and Joshua xv. 14–19, the
agreement is almost verbatim. On the other hand,
Judges i. 21 reads, " And the children of Benjamin
did not drive out the Jebusites that inhabited Jerusalem, but the Jebusites dwelt with the children of
Benjamin in Jerusalem, unto this day ; " while Joshua
xv. 63 declares, " As for the Jebusites, the inhabitants of Jerusalem, the children of Judah could not
drive them out, but the Jebusites dwelt with the children of Judah at Jerusalem unto this day." According to both narratives, Jebus was not captured until
a later period ; but according to one account it was
due to the remissness of the Benjaminites, and in the

other to that of the Judeans. The difference between
Judges i. 29 and Joshua xvi. 10 illustrates the different concepts of the history entertained by the authors
of the two books. According to Judges, the Canaanites are not driven out from Gezer, but retain their
independence in the midst of the Hebrews ; while in
Joshua they are represented as being at once reduced
to bondage, — a bondage which we know was first in-
stituted in the reign of Solomon (sect. 149). The
important fact to be noted is that the oldest passages in both books clearly state that the tribes of the
north and of the south struggled separately for their
territory, and then at first succeeded only partially in
conquering it.

34. In the second and greater section, Judges ii. 6–
xvi. 31, appear the traces of the work of a later editor,
whose language, ideas, and spirit are very similar to
that of the author of Deuteronomy. Because of this
fact, and to distinguish him from the other writers
whose work is preserved in the books of Judges,
Samuel, and Kings, he is commonly designated " the
Deuteronomic editor." A characteristic product of
his pen is the recurring formula already referred to
(sect. 32), — suffering ; bondage ; penitence ; deliverance ; peace. The greater part of the introduction to
the second section (ii. 6–iii. 6) is also evidently from
the hand of the same writer. But chapter ii. 6–9 is
repeated almost word for word from Joshua xxiv. 28,
31, 29, 30. Chapter ii. 11–19 presents the theory of
the Deuteronomic editor respecting the period of the
judges. Two different reasons are suggested in the
passages — ii. 22, iii. 4, and iii. 1–3 — why the Canaanites were not utterly exterminated. In the first it

was that Israel might be tested, to determine whether
or not she would keep the commandments of Jehovah;
in the second it was that she might have constant practice in the art of war. These and other indications
of different points of view are clearly due to the incorporation of material from different sources. It is
probable that iii. 1–3, which is the oldest section, originally followed immediately after chapter i. The work
of the Deuteronomic editor is further manifest in
Judges iii. 7–15ᵃ, 39ᵇ; iv. 1–3; v. 31ᵇ; vi. 1, 7–10;
viii. 27ᵇ, 33–35; x. 6, 17; xiii. 1; xv. 20; xvi. 31ᵇ,
— as the recurring phrases and thought peculiar to
him demonstrate. The difference between his conceptions and the testimony of the ancient narratives,
as might be expected, is often very great. He, for
example, conceives of the judges as ruling over all
Israel, while the older authorities disclose the fact
that their rule was only local. Also the intensely
religious spirit which he breathes into this savage age
was not born until the prophets had preached for
generations.

35. The earlier portions of Judges present some interesting examples of parallel narrative. The older poetical
record of the victory over the Canaanites gained under
the leadership of Deborah and Barak, preserved in
chapter v., is paralleled by the prose narrative of chapter iv. Although evidently transmitted through independent channels and coming from different eras, both
are old and agree in general outlines. The later
editor finding both incorporated them, and in so doing
introduced certain minor differences. In chapter v.,
for example, Sisera is at the head of the combination
of kings (v. 20), and his mother is attended (v. 28) by

princesses; while in chapter iv. Jabin is the king of
Canaan reigning at Hazor, and Sisera is only his general. In the poem it is practically stated that both
Deborah and Barak belong to the tribe of Issachar
(v. 15); while according to the prose narrative Deborah
is of the tribe of Ephraim (iv. 5) and Barak from Naphtali (iv. 6). According to the representation of v. 27,
Jael struck down Sisera as he was standing, else he
would not " bow and fall and lie at her feet;" -but
iv. 21 states that she drove a tent-pin through his head
as he lay asleep.

36. Clear indications of the presence of two accounts of the victory of Gideon (Jerubbaal) over the
Midianites are also noticeable. Between verses 3 and
4 of chapter viii. there is a break. In vii. 25 the
Ephraimites are represented as bringing the heads of
the slain Midianite kings to Gideon beyond Jordan.
But in viii. 4 Gideon comes to the Jordan, and then
crosses it for the first time. In viii. 1–3 the victory
has already been won, and in the division of the spoil
the jealousy of the Ephraimites is allayed only by the
conciliatory words of Gideon. According to vii. 23
and 24, Gideon had raised a huge levy among the
tribes; but in viii. 4 there is no suggestion of a great
victory. Gideon with only three hundred men is in
pursuit of the Midianites. Furthermore, the refusal
of the people of Succoth and Penuel (viii. 5–9) to
give him food is not at all in keeping with the treatment usually accorded to a conqueror. Evidently,
viii. 4 introduces us into the middle of the second
narrative; the first part has been lost, and the facts
can be gleaned only from what remains. In many ways
these two narratives admirably illustrate the differences

between the earlier and later points of view. According to the testimony of chapter viii., Gideon with a little band of three hundred (his immediate retainers, the
Abiezerites, whom he has hastily summoned) is in hot
pursuit of two Midian kings. Across the Jordan and
out upon the great caravan route he follows, until he
overtakes and captures them. Then the reason which
prompted his attack is disclosed. According to the
confession of the Midianite kings (verse 18), in one of
their incursions near Tabor they had slain his two
brothers. Consequently, the relentless law of blood
revenge — considered by the ancient Semites even
more sacred than an obligation to the deity — impelled
this prince of Northern Israel to perform the bold act
which brought him so prominently before his countrymen and subsequently led to his election as king.
With the other narrative, which is written from the
religious point of view, we are familiar. This represents Gideon as one of the humblest of all Israel, and
as acting merely as a passive instrument in the hand
of Jehovah. The great religious truths which the
prophet sought thereby to teach have become the
possession of humanity.

But for the historic purpose the question must be
raised, Which narrative is the older and consequently
presents the historical facts? That the ruder, the
more natural, and the one most in harmony with
the savage age is the older and more exact cannot
be questioned for a moment. This conclusion is confirmed even by a superficial examination of the first
narrative (vi. 1–viii. 3). Here the statements are
somewhat conflicting. Certain verses suggest that
the tribes of Manasseh, Asher, Zebulon, and Naphtali

were summoned by Gideon and responded to his call in great numbers; but running through the same section is a series of verses which consistently with the earlier narrative (viii. 4–21) represent Gideon as collecting the Abiezerites (vi. 34), and with them alone winning the victory (viii. 2), which aroused the envy of the warlike Ephraimites. The reference in vi. 1– viii. 3 to the faithful three hundred who accompanied him agrees with the account of the three hundred retainers of the tribe of Abiezer, with whom, according to viii. 4–24, he attacked the Midianites. Thus again the older sections of both accounts are in accord. Therefore it is evident that upon the older narrative (viii. 4–21) the structure of Hebrew history must be reared. The other account may contain references to some subsequent victory. If its date can be determined, it also becomes at once a valuable source of information concerning the religious thought of the later period from whence it came and whose ideas it reflects.

37. The third section of the Book of Judges, chapters xvii.–xxi., is an appendix recording certain incidents in this period. Chapters xvii. and xviii. tell of the migration of the Danites, and of the establishment of the sanctuary at Dan. The system of morality which this section sets forth is exceedingly primitive. The material doubtless is very old. Chapter xix. likewise bears the stamp of antiquity. Chapters xx. and xxi. on the contrary abound in ideas peculiar to a very much later age, and contain many statements which it is impossible to reconcile with the information furnished by the earlier records. The kernel of historic fact has evidently grown luxuriantly during the long

period of oral transmission.   The little Book of Ruth
also might properly be included in this appendix, since
through it we are introduced (although by a writer
living much later) to the primitive life of this early
epoch.

38. The period of the judges extends to the establishment of the monarchy.   Consequently, I. Samuel
1–7, which tells of the boyhood of Samuel, the history
of the sanctuary at Shiloh, and the defeat of the Hebrews by the Philistines, is also one of its historical
sources.   Here again the work of redaction is apparent.   In the oldest section (iv. 1–vii. 1), which records
the disastrous battle of Aphek and the subsequent
capture of the Ark by the Philistines, attention is
focused upon Northern Israel, and the subjects treated
are of national interest.   The connection between
the preceding chapters and this section is not close.
In the former the theme of chief interest is the
seer Samuel.   This may well have been added subsequently, as an introduction to chapters iv. 1–vii. 1.
The shorter passage (ii. 27–36) was evidently inserted
still later, since it breaks the close connection between
ii. 26 and iii. 1.   Its language and thought also are
different, and are in the spirit of the Deuteronomic
editor whose work appeared in Judges (sect. 34).   A
similar transition is manifest in vii. 2–17.   The events
therein recorded are incompatible with what is known
of the Hebrews before and after this date.   As a matter of fact the Philistine yoke, instead of being completely thrown off, continued to rest still more heavily
upon the afflicted Hebrews.   The latter remained the
serfs, not the masters.   The religious tone of the passage and the nature of its thought stamp it as the

product of some late prophetic writer.   Therefore
these opening chapters of I. Samuel, like the Book
of Judges, are composed of early and late sections
loosely bound together.   In reconstructing the history, the relative age of the sources and the point of
view from which they were written will constantly
be considered.

II

SETTLEMENT AND FINAL LOCATION OF THE
HEBREW TRIBES

39. How long the victorious Israelitish tribes remained in their newly acquired possessions on the east-Jordan headlands cannot be definitely determined. Moses, their great leader, died during this period, and a new generation came to the front. The conquest of the Amorite kingdom worked mighty changes in the character and life of the wandering tribes, who now became agriculturists instead of nomads. A quieter mode of living, a settled abode, and a sufficient means of subsistence insured a longer life. A great increase in the number of offspring, which always appears when a nomadic people become agricultural, also added rapidly to the numbers of the Israelites. Their limited territory soon proved insufficient for their needs. Behind them, attacking and constantly pressing in upon them, were the Arab tribes from the desert, who were ever eager for the spoils if not the toils of the more fruitful lands which had been occupied by their former companions. To pressure from within and without was added the temptation presented by the conditions in Canaan; for just at this time the rule of the Egyptians and Hittites had relaxed, and each city and tribe had asserted its independence. Palestinian politics were a chaotic jumble. The strong cities of the plain were able for centuries to resist foreign invasion; but the

less desirable land up among the mountains had not as
yet been occupied, and therefore was open to the first
comer. Canaan was by no means an unpromising field
for the immigrant.

40. Erelong, the Hebrews began to cross the Jordan
just above the Dead Sea. Jericho, " the city of palms "
(Deut. xxxiv. 3), which was most exposed to attack
from the east, first fell into their hands. In the old
record in Judges (i. 16) the Kenites are mentioned as
going up with the tribe of Judah from " the city of
palm-trees." This fact indicates, perhaps, that the
Kenites united with the Israelites in the capture of
Jericho, or else had become masters of it at an earlier
date, — just as had their kinsmen, the Kenizzites, of
Hebron and Debir. At Gilgal, whose name " circle "
marks it as a sacred place among the ancient Canaanites, was deposited the Ark, that holy symbol of Jehovah's presence which during the wilderness wandering
had been the religious centre and consequently the
common standard of all the allied Hebrew tribes. From
this point, which connected and commanded both the
east and west, the tribe of Judah, accompanied by the
Simeonites and their nomadic allies the Kenites (Judges
i. 16), first went up to conquer for themselves a territory in southern Canaan (Judges i. 3). The accounts
of their conquest are very meagre. Constrained by
the common danger, the petty rulers of the towns thus
menaced united under the leadership of one of their
kings, Adoni-bezek. At his capital town a battle was
fought. The wild energy of a brave, rude people was
matched against the effete civilization of Canaan, and
the former won the day. The captured king suffered
the cruelties which the Israelites, as well as the other

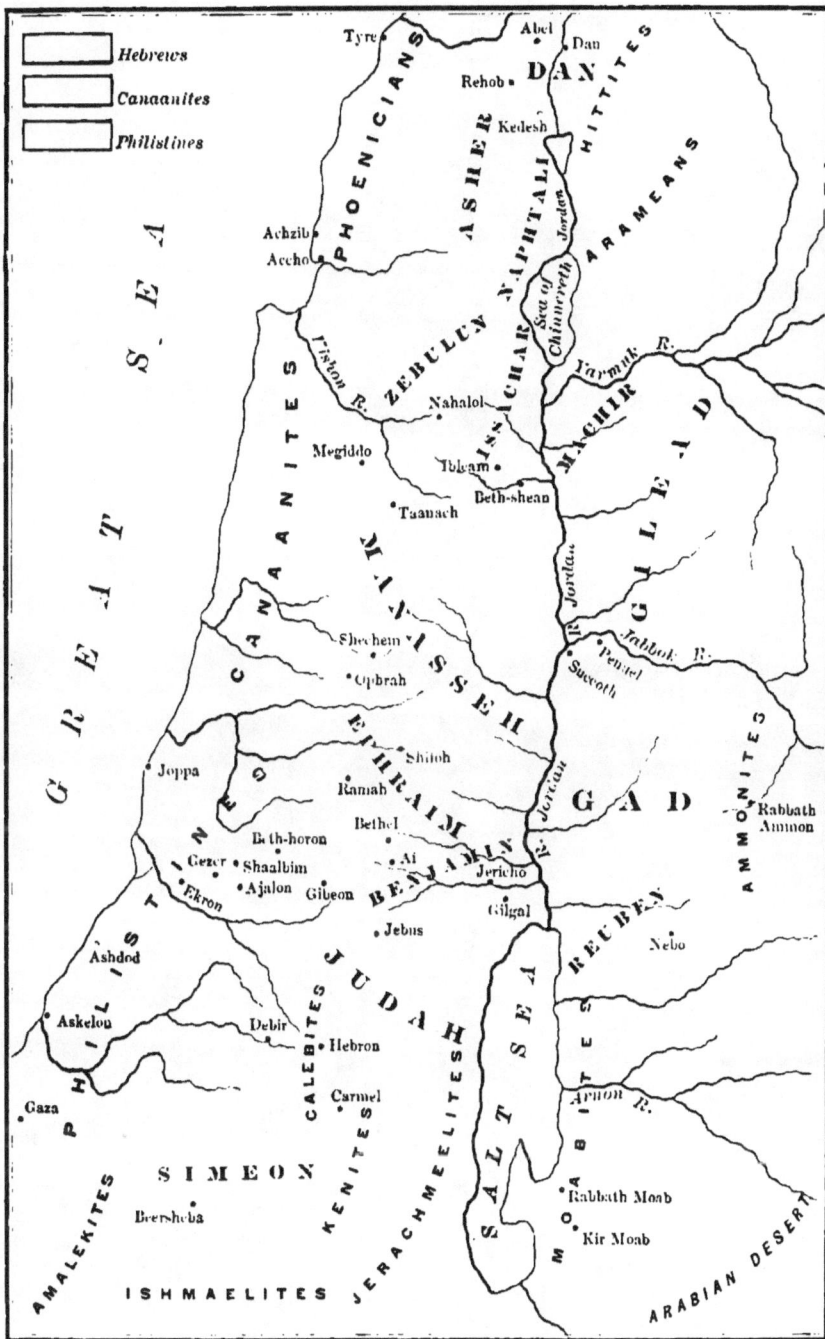

TERRITORIAL DIVISION OF CANAAN AFTER THE CONQUEST.

barbarous people with whom they associated, inflicted upon their fallen foes.

The conquests of the Judeans were only gradual and partial, being confined to the hill country where they could fight on more favorable terms. The plains, on which chariots and horses could be used, remained in the hands of the Canaanites (Judges i. 19). In fact, it appears that the Hebrews in the south won their land more by alliance and intermarriage with the Arab peoples dwelling there than by the sword. They found the Calebites in possession of Hebron, which they had wrested from its earlier inhabitants (Joshua xv. 14). Debir was the capital of the tribe of Othniel (Judges i. 12, 13 ; Joshua xv. 17). With these local clans, as with the Kenites, they entered into the closest relations, gradually absorbing them with their territory. These southern tribes probably, like the Israelites, had come originally from the desert. In the older records their genealogy is traced back to the Edomites. Caleb and Othniel are spoken of as sons of Kenaz (Num. xxxii. 12; Joshua xiv. 6, 14 ; Judges iii. 9, 10). The tribe of Kenaz or the Kenizzites are mentioned among the early inhabitants of Canaan (Gen. xv. 19) side by side with the Kenites, who from the first affiliated with the Hebrews. In Genesis xxxvi. 11, 15, 42, the Kenizzites are reckoned among the Edomites. In this early period they appear as nomadic tribes, passing over, like the Hebrews, from the wandering life of the desert to seek homes in southern Palestine. A common language, civilization, and aim made their assimilation especially easy. As a result, the blood of the southern Hebrew tribes was diluted with many foreign elements. On the north also the stronghold of

Jebus retained its independence down to the days of David. Extending westward from Jebus, across the central plateau of Palestine, was the zone of Canaanitish cities, — Har-heres, Gezer, Aijalon, and Shaalbim, — which completely cut off the southern Israelites from those of the north (Judges i. 35). Hence they were obliged to fight their battles alone, and to solve their own problems. Their early history is as independent of that of their northern kinsmen as if the latter had not existed.

41. From Jericho, the northern tribes likewise went up at a subsequent date to secure a home for themselves in Canaan. This great northern invasion was headed by the house of Joseph (Judges i. 22), which was accompanied by the tribes of Benjamin, Zebulon, Naphtali, Issachar, and Asher. Although his name is not mentioned in the ancient record preserved in Judges i., there is no sufficient reason for doubting that their leader was Joshua. By stratagem and sudden attack they became masters of the important Canaanitish towns of Ai and Bethel, before the inhabitants of the land were aroused. Near the town of Gibeon, with which the Israelites had made a friendly treaty, a great battle was fought, which gave them possession of the highlands of central Ephraim. The eleventh chapter of Joshua tells of another successful battle near the waters of Merom, against the allied Canaanite kings of the north, led by Jabin, king of Hazor. If these victories were as great as recorded, generations nevertheless passed before the Hebrews became the real masters of the land. It is significant that the ancient narrative in Judges is chiefly occupied in recapitulating the towns which remained in the hands of the Canaanites. Sub-

sequent history confirms this record. Across the fertile
plain of Esdraelon from the Jordan to the great sea
extended another zone of Canaanitish cities, including
Bethshean, Taanach, Dor, Ibleam, Megiddo, and their
tributary towns (Judges i. 27), which completely separated the tribes of Ephraim, Manasseh, and Benjamin
from their more northern kinsmen. Scattered through
the territory of the Israelites north of the plain of
Esdraelon, occupying the most fertile plains, were a
multitude of strong Canaanitish cities. The Hebrew
immigrants at the beginning of the period of the judges
held only a few towns (Jericho, Ai, Bethel, and Hebron)
and the least desirable rocky, mountainous regions. In
addition they were divided and separated from one
another by seemingly impassable barriers.

42. When the initial impetus of the conquest lost
its force, the Canaanites were still masters of the land.
Not all at once nor by the sword alone did the Israelites become possessed of that heritage which was theirs
to win. Intermarriage with the Canaanitish peoples
became exceedingly common when they finally settled
down peaceably side by side. Blood covenants were
also established between the Israelites and friendly
tribes. The general disintegration of the Canaanitish
peoples fostered this process of assimilation. While
the Judeans in the south were gradually absorbing the
Kenites, the Calebites, and the Jerachmeelites, the Hebrews in the north were fusing with the native populations there. In the Canaanitish town of Shechem, for
example, Israelites and Canaanites are found living together, and even sharing the same temple and nominally
worshipping the same god, who was significantly called
" Baal of the covenant " (Judges ix. 1–5). In some

parts of the land Canaanitish — in others, Israelitish —
influence was the stronger. The great problem was
which would conquer in the end. Certainly the Canaanites, with their superior civilization, enjoyed a
great advantage; in fact, they taught the new-comers
all that they knew of agriculture and the arts. But
the problem was not merely a political and social one;
it was likewise religious. Would the Israelites also
accept the religion of their teachers and masters? The
future of the Hebrew tribes at the beginning of the
period of the judges was far from bright. Never bound
together very closely, they were now divided and busily
engaged each in securing a place of abode and in making
a home. Insidious dangers lurked in their midst, and
formidable foes without were watching an opportunity
to assail them. Their own religious concepts and moral
standards were by no means the highest. A mighty
and persistent force — a force not human but divine
— was required to evolve a nation out of this seeming chaos.

43. The exact location of the Hebrew tribes after
their final settlement in Canaan is not definitely established. The importance of these tribal divisions does
not, in fact, appear to have been nearly as great as is
popularly supposed. Simple addition quickly demonstrates that the division into twelve tribes is not exact,
since thirteen distinct tribes sought a home in Palestine. Counting the half-tribe of Manasseh, which in
size and strength surpassed some entire tribes, there
were fourteen. Many sub-tribes — such as Abiezer,
Suph, and Machir — figure even more prominently in
Hebrew history than certain of the smaller general
divisions: as, for example, Simeon and Reuben.

44. In the south the strong tribe of Judah occupied the central plateau. Their territory extended from the Dead Sea to the Philistine plain, and from Jebus in the north to the desert on the south. Living in their midst and affiliating with them were many from the scattered tribe of Levi. On their southern borders, extending out into the Judean wilderness, were settled the remnants of the Simeonites. The early fortunes of the tribes of Levi and Simeon are dimly suggested in the old song preserved in Genesis xlix. 5–7, where they are bitterly condemned for their treachery and violence. Some deed of perfidy and wantonness is hinted at which aroused the righteous indignation of their kinsmen : —

> Cursed be their anger, for it was fierce;
> And their wrath, for it was cruel.

The punishment for their crime is also referred to in general terms : —

> I will divide them in Jacob,
> And scatter them in Israel.

Nowhere in the Old Testament is the exact nature of the deed which brought down upon these two tribes their dire retribution revealed, unless it be alluded to in the thirty-fourth chapter of Genesis. According to the representation of that strange passage, the Israelites entered into a close alliance with the Canaanites dwelling at Shechem, sealing it by intermarriage. Thus the two peoples were bound together by the closest and most sacred bonds known to the Semitic world. Treacherously taking advantage of the confidence which these relations inspired, Simeon and Levi, with their swords, "came upon the city not fearing

5

danger and slew all the males" (Gen. xxxiv. 25);
then they proceeded to spoil the city, reaping the fruits
of their duplicity. This deed, as recorded, agrees
well with the sin darkly shadowed in Genesis xlix.
It called forth a cry of horror from Israel: "Simeon
and Levi, ye have troubled me, to bring me into ill
odor among the inhabitants of the land, among the
Canaanites and Perizzites" (xxxiv. 30). With the
condemnation was closely associated a fear lest the
Canaanites should arise and destroy them all in revenge for this base crime of the Simeonites and
Levites. The two feelings of indignation and fear
were thus united in the minds of the Israelites, impelling them to leave their kinsmen to their fate. The
incensed Canaanites would not be slow to act. That
some such retribution overtook the tribes of Simeon
and Levi at an early stage in the Hebrew occupation
of Canaan is in perfect agreement with the passage in
Genesis xlix. already referred to, and with the little
that we know of them in later times. The Simeonites,
living on the borders of the desert, gradually reverted
to their former nomadic life and were absorbed by the
wandering Arabian tribes, so that they soon almost
completely disappeared from Hebrew history. In the
ancient annals of the Book of Judges, wandering
Levites are incidentally mentioned as living among
the different tribes (xvii. 7, 9, 12; xviii. 15, 30; xix. 1).
At this early date they are completely scattered, and
already the tendency to turn over to them the charge
of the sanctuaries and ceremonial rites is apparent.

45. The "House of Joseph" was the dominant
power in the north. It included the strong tribes of
Ephraim and Manasseh, who occupied the fertile hill-

country lying south of the plain of Esdraelon and extending to the Jordan on the east and the coast plains on the west. The Benjaminites were a smaller branch of these northern tribes, who found a home in the rugged hills which lay between Ephraim and Judah. The rich plain of Esdraelon was occupied in time by the tribe of Issachar, while the rolling hills to the north became the possession of the tribe of Zebulon. The long, narrow strip of land extending from the plain of Esdraelon to the foot of the Lebanons, skirting the Jordan, was the home of the Naphtalites. The tribe of Asher settled on the western slopes of that elevated plateau which was known in later times as Upper Galilee. These northern tribes were never very strong, and the older inhabitants of the land were so firmly intrenched that they almost completely absorbed the Hebrew immigrants, who were so far removed from the heart of Israel. It was not until that heart began to beat vigorously under David, and to send its pulsations of national life to the extremities, that they became in reality an active part of the commonwealth.

46. On the southwestern slopes of Mount Ephraim, the Danites, who in Judges xviii. 11 are styled not a tribe but a family, originally settled. The populous tribe of Ephraim pressed them from behind, while out on the plain they were obliged to contest the soil with the powerful native inhabitants. The Song of Deborah refers to the Danites as "remaining by their ships" (Judges v. 17), which indicates that at that time their territory touched the sea. But the first chapter of Judges (verses 34, 35) states that the Amorites forced them back into the hill country, and

also continued to occupy the chief towns in their territory, — Har-heres, Aijalon, and Shaalbim.   The term
" Amorites " seems to have been loosely applied to the
native inhabitants of the land.   Probably the foes of
the Danites were the Philistines, whose power was
in the ascendency during the latter part of the period of
the judges.   The seventeenth and eighteenth chapters
of Judges contain a very old and authentic narrative,
which throws light upon the subsequent history of the
Danites, and at the same time illustrates the experiences of the Hebrews in acquiring a place of abode.
Finding their quarters too narrow, they sought a home
elsewhere.   In their search they had the sympathy of
the other tribes.   The five men sent out as spies consult first the priest of a certain Ephraimite concerning
the next step in their history; then they proceed up
the Jordan valley, until at the foot of Mount Hermon
they find a retired spot occupied by a peaceful Phœnician colony, far removed from the parent state.
When they report to their tribesmen, six hundred
warriors set out at once; on the way they steal the
priest of the Ephraimite and his religious parapher-
nalia.   The Phœnician city falls an easy prey to their
arms.   Its name is changed to Dan, and a tribal sanctuary is established, over which the stolen priest pre-
sides.   This henceforth became the real home of the
Danites ; if any remained in the south, they were too
few and insignificant to figure in subsequent history.
In Deuteronomy xxxiii. 22, Dan is referred to as a
" lion's whelp that leapeth forth from Bashan."   Being
removed from the rest of the tribes and at the same
time exposed to attack from northern invaders, they
were often called upon to defend themselves.   The

forty-ninth chapter of Genesis already quoted, describes Dan as a serpent in the way and as an adder in the path, that biteth the horse's heels so that his rider falleth backwards (verse 17), — indicating the character of the guerilla warfare to which they were obliged to resort and in which they became adept.

47. On the elevated plateaus of Gilead in the east-Jordan territory, certain of the Manassite clans found a home. Their most prominent family, that of Machir, sent representatives to support the common Hebrew cause in the grand rally under Deborah and Barak (Judges v. 14). Their territory was productive and their numbers great; so that although separated from their tribesmen in Canaan and surrounded by hostile neighbors, they succeeded in maintaining their independence by their swords. Farther south, between the Jordan and the territory of the Ammonites, were located the Gadites. According to Numbers xxxii. 34–36, their territory extended southward to the Arnon, the boundary of Moab in the time of Hebrew supremacy. The cities attributed to the Reubenites (Num. xxxii. 37, 38) were located immediately east of the northern end of the Dead Sea, and therefore within the limits of Gad. All the biblical references indicate the weakness of the Reubenites. At the time when the Israelites rallied to throw off the Canaanitish yoke, although they recognized their obligation to respond, they sat like cowards among their sheepfolds (Judges v. 15, 16). The old song preserved in Deuteronomy xxxiii. reads (verse 6): —

> Let Reuben live and die not;
> Yet let his numbers be few.

Few they certainly were, little more than a clan of the Gadites. Before the establishment of the kingdom it is difficult to determine where they made their home; and although the Moabite stone records the conquest by the Moabites of the cities assigned in Numbers to the Reubenites, it makes no reference to their existence. Like the Simeonites, they seem to have reverted to their former nomadic life, or else to have been absorbed by the neighboring clans. The Gadites, however, maintained themselves, at least in the northern part of their territory, and gained a reputation for their fierce courage: —

> Gad, a marauding band shall press upon him;
> But he shall press upon their heel.[1]

> Blessed be he that enlargeth Gad:
> He dwelleth as a lioness,
> And teareth the arm, yea, the crown of the head.[2]

These sententious allusions tell the story of the long intermittent war which was the price at which the Gadites retained their homes and lands.

[1] Gen. xlix. 19.   [2] Deut. xxxiii. 20.

III

48. THE Deuteronomic editor of the book, which is the great historical source for this period, seems to conceive of the judges as ruling over all the tribes, and following one another in regular succession. It is obvious that under the existing conditions such unity of action was unknown, in reality impossible. The united testimony of the earlier narratives corroborates this conclusion. The conception of the Deuteronomic editor was the result of the natural tendency to read back into this formative, pioneer period the conditions of his own time, when the rule and regular succession of the kings was established. The judges were begotten by the necessities of their age and environment. A common danger — most frequently an invasion — threatened a town or tribe. At such a critical moment as this, some man of superior courage, energy, or wisdom arose, and rallying his tribesmen led them out to victory. Having thus demonstrated his ability to act and command, he was naturally regarded as their deliverer and head. His authority was derived from no constitution, but was voluntarily delegated by the people under the pressure of a common need. As a result, his power was sometimes very slight; and in other cases it approximated to that of a military dictator. In that turbulent, chaotic world differences

71

frequently arose between individuals and clans, which under the dominance of the relentless laws of blood-revenge led to the most disastrous consequences. The need of some arbiter whose wisdom and authority both parties could trust was strongly felt. Hence, as a mere incident of the situation, such cases as these were frequently referred for decision to the victorious champion. This fact probably led later writers to use the term "judge" (*shophat*) to designate these local chieftains. "Deliverer" or "saviour," the appellation found in the ancient narratives, describes much more accurately their character and functions. Their rule usually was confined to a small territory. In some cases it was limited to a local clan, and at most it did not extend beyond three or four tribes associated together by virtue of location or common danger; any political organization which they may have formed dissolved at their death. Respecting some of these champions, little more than the remembrance of their name has been preserved. In the south, Ehud was the deliverer from Moabite incursion; Samson and Shamgar were leaders against the Philistines. Among the northern and central tribes, living probably in part contemporaneously with the heroes of the south, were Deborah, Barak, and Tola of the tribe of Issachar, and Gideon the Manassite. Among the deliverers of the east-Jordan tribes were the two Gileadites, Jair and Jephthah. Undoubtedly there were many others who were as prominent as some of those whose names have been preserved by the flash-light pictures of the Book of Judges.

49. The work of some of these champions was very ephemeral. Pre-eminently is this true of that of Sam-

son. There are too many local touches, reflecting the
peculiarities of the rocky headlands of western Judah
and of the period to which he is assigned, to allow one
to find in the traditions which have gathered about the
name of this old hero merely localized sun-myths. It
would be strange indeed if many later accretions had
not partially enveloped him in mist; but even these
are of value, since they reveal the impressions which
his personality made upon later generations. In this
dim light it is clear that he was a characteristic product of his age. Impetuous, wily, vindictive, ruled by
his passions, he was a physical giant but a moral weak-
ling. The blows which he struck against the foes of
his country were the blows of a child, impulsive and
without the persistent character which is the index of
a lofty purpose. His deeds of strength and daring
made a deep impression upon an age which worshipped brute force ; but as a result of his life-work
his kinsmen were no nearer deliverance from Philistine
incursions.

50. The activity of Ehud the Benjaminite was far
more fruitful. While the Israelites and Moabites always recognized their kinship, this never deterred either
from invading the territory of the other as occasion
offered. When the tide of immigration swept across
the Jordan and up over the central plateau of Palestine,
it left the eastern outposts exposed. Each tribe and
family, intent upon subduing their own land, found no
time for wars of common defence. This opportunity
— under an energetic leader, Eglon — the Moabites improved, seizing the not easily defended city of Jericho,
and laying tribute upon the adjacent territory. Then
it was that Ehud, one of the Israelitish chieftains, gain-

ing an audience with the Moabite king, treacherously slew him. Escaping, he summoned the Ephraimites and succeeded in driving the Moabites back to the east of the Jordan, — thus securing deliverance for the Israelites, whose territory had been menaced. Throughout the remainder of the period of the judges the tribes of the south do not again emerge into prominence. Having absorbed the strongest local clans, they were more completely masters of the land than those of the north; at the same time, the strength of the common bond which bound them together was weakened. As has been noted, natural and political barriers also separated them from their northern kinsmen and shut them in to themselves. Hence the division between the tribes of the north and south took definite form with the settlement in Canaan.

51. In the north, all the energy of the Israelites was devoted to conquering the uplands which had fallen to their lot. Meantime the strong, independent Canaanitish cities on the plain of Esdraelon and in the north were united under a king by the name of Sisera. He introduced a systematic policy of repression, whereby he sought to separate and subdue the scattered Hebrew immigrants. One by one they were disarmed and subjugated. In the language of that song which is the oldest and most authentic record concerning this early period, —

> In the days of Jael the highways were in disuse,
> And the travellers walked through bypaths:
> The villages in Israel were unoccupied.[1]

Deliberate misgovernment was reducing the land to its primitive desolation. Subjugation to the Canaanites

[1] Judges v. 6, 7.

also meant in time the universal dominance of their religion, and consequently the abandonment of the worship of Jehovah. Already, in the language of the old
song, " The people were choosing new gods." It was
an important crisis in Hebrew history. The deliverer
was a woman, Deborah the prophetess, one of the ma-
trons in Israel. She was the worthy predecessor of
Samuel; apparently, her religious zeal and spiritual
insight had already secured for her a position of influence among the Israelites; her divine enlightenment
enabled her to appreciate the real significance of the
danger which impended. Something must be done,
and that quickly. Accordingly, she calls upon Barak,
the son of Ahinoam, a prominent chief of the north
who had himself experienced the rigors of Canaanite
oppression (Judges v. 12), to rally the tribes for a
struggle. She readily accords with Barak's request
that she co-operate with him, since her " heart is toward
the leaders of Israel who offered themselves willingly
among the people" (Judges v. 9). Common kinship
is not the strongest bond uniting the Israelites, since
they had already freely intermarried with the Canaanites; it is rather their common faith in Jehovah.
The name of Jehovah stood for national liberty; he
had delivered them from Egypt; the covenant with
him had held together the tribes during the long
desert wandering. Now, in the name of Jehovah, Deborah and Barak arouse the Hebrews to united action:

Hear, O ye kings! give ear, O ye princes!
I, even I, will sing unto Jehovah;
I will sing praise to Jehovah, the God of Israel.
Jehovah, when thou wentest forth out of Seir,
When thou marchedst out of the field of Edom,

The earth trembled, the heavens also dropped,
Yea, the clouds dropped water.
The mountains quaked at the presence of Jehovah,
Even yon Sinai at the presence of Jehovah, the God of Israel.[1]

The tribes of Ephraim, Manasseh, Benjamin, Zebulon, Issachar, Naphtali, and the east-Jordan clan of Machir respond to the rallying cry of Deborah and Barak. Forty thousand in all came up "to the help of Jehovah against the mighty." The Reubenites and Gileadites recognize the call to duty, but they hesitate until their courage fails them. Dan and Asher, having caught the spirit of their neighbors the Phœnicians, are selfishly intent upon commerce only. Judah and Simeon are not even mentioned among the Israelitish tribes.

52. The Song of Deborah, with a few bold fresco strokes, paints the battle-scene. The Canaanitish army is drawn up on the plain of Esdraelon, northeast of Mount Carmel, near the lower waters of the Kishon. The advantage of the position is all with them, since near by are their strong cities; and here their chariots can be used most effectively. The Hebrew army, according to the prose narrative, first rally near Mount Tabor; thence they march southward out upon the great plain. Against the well-equipped and disciplined host of the Canaanites rush the Israelitish peasants, impelled by the religious zeal and patriotic enthusiasm which had been kindled by the inspired prophetess of Jehovah. The references to "the stars fighting in their courses against Sisera" and the flooded Kishon, interpreted from poetry into prose, suggest a sudden and heavy rainfall. This would quickly render the plain — which is level, and in consequence of the nature of the

[1] Judges v. 3-5.

soil very susceptible to rain — too muddy for the ma-
nœuvring of chariots. The "stamping of the horses'
hoofs" and "the plunging of their strong ones," which
are reflected in the old poem, confirm this conclusion.
Such a storm, so fatal to the Canaanitish cause and so
favorable to that of the Hebrews, would by the contestants be recognized as a direct intervention of Israel's
God. The experience of the exodus is renewed; Jehovah is manifesting himself with might to deliver his
people. The Hebrew peasants are inspired with an
irresistible courage, while their foes are dismayed and
terrified. Into the flooded Kishon the shattered remnants of the Canaanitish army are driven, to be carried
away by its muddy waters. Among the few who escape
is their leader, Sisera. Unattended, he flees northward
until he reaches the tent of one of those wandering
Kenites who had assimilated so readily with the Israelites. Trusting to the laws of treaty and hospitality, he
enters and seeks refuge; but his trust is misplaced. By
the hand of Jael, the wife of the Kenite whose tent he
has entered, he falls. Thus in the eyes of the Semitic
world the superlative of ignominy is heaped upon the
oppressor of the Hebrews.

53. The results of this sweeping victory were far-
reaching. In northern Israelitish history it was the
great war of independence. Instead of the galling
yoke of Canaanitish bondage, the tribes of the north
secured freedom; the serfs suddenly became the masters. The power of the Canaanites was forever broken,
and the territory of central Palestine was thrown open
to the immigrants. Above all, the Hebrews had learned
the all-important lesson that union meant deliverance
and the mastery over their foes. The importance of

that bond which had united them, the common faith in Jehovah their God, was realized as never before. It was, therefore, a religious as well as a political victory. Jehovah by this act again revealed himself to his people as a God able and willing to deliver. Consequently, he continued to command their trust even though so many circumstances conspired to shake it.

IV

ORIGIN AND HISTORY OF THE KINGDOM
OF GIDEON

54. THE victory won and the common danger averted, the Israelites went back to their homes. Barak and Deborah in time passed away, and no leader or organization bound the tribes together. After the conquest of the strong cities on the plain of Esdraelon, its broad fields were left exposed. A wide valley leads up to it from the Jordan and the desert beyond. As the seasons rolled around they brought from the great Arabian desert marauding bands of the Midianites, bent upon reaping the products of these fruitful fields. Ill-organized efforts to defend their possessions gave little relief to the Hebrews from their ruthless, wily foes. By degrees they were disarmed and reduced to a most galling serfdom; they began to realize that they had only exchanged the Canaanitish for the Midianite yoke. Again they sighed for a deliverer. A seeming accident called him forth. In one of their plundering forays, a band of the Midianites penetrated to the vicinity of Mount Tabor to the north of Esdraelon; there they were resisted by men of the sub-tribe of Abiezer. In the skirmish some of the Hebrews were slain. Among others were the brothers of a certain Jerubbaal, better known to later generations as Gideon ("The Hewer"). The sacred law of blood-revenge imperatively commanded him to avenge this deed.

Gathering a small band, three hundred of his household retainers, he set out to overtake the marauders and slay the princes whose hands had been stained with his brothers' blood. Directly eastward from their home at Ophrah they hastened down to the Jordan and across it in hot pursuit. Faint and hungry, they demanded food from the inhabitants of Succoth and Penuel. Fear of the Midianites led the elders of these Israelitish towns to refuse to their kinsmen the needed succor. With a vow to take vengeance upon them on his return, Gideon and his little band hurried onward upon the great desert highway. Not suspecting pursuit, the Midianites were not on their guard. The brave few fell upon them unexpectedly, and putting the band to flight captured their two princes. Gideon's first act was to take summary vengeance upon the inhospitable towns of Succoth and Penuel; then he was at liberty to accomplish that deed for which he set out upon his bold expedition. Unhesitatingly, the two Midianite kings who had been captured declare in answer to his question that near Mount Tabor they slew certain Hebrews who resembled their captor. Whether or not they suspected that they were speaking to the brother of their victims is not clear, but their words are their condemnation; the law of blood-revenge demanded their blood to avenge that of Gideon's murdered brothers. When, notwithstanding his father's command, the youthful son of Gideon hesitated to smite the Midianite chiefs, the prince of the Abiezerites relentlessly cut them down, and his sacred obligation was fulfilled.

55. On Gideon's return as victor to Ophrah, the Israelites of central Canaan recognized in him the deliverer

for whom they had eagerly longed. They began also to appreciate the disadvantages of the intermittent rule of the judges, and accordingly said to him, "Rule thou over us, both thou and thy son, and thy son's son also." Thus simply and naturally was the idea of the kingship introduced into Hebrew life. According to the narrative, the conquering hero modestly refused their offer; but acts speak louder than words in the past as well as the present. With the gold of the spoils captured from the Midianites, he proceeded at once to make an ephod. This image, overlaid with gold, he set up at his home and future capital, Ophrah, thereby making this the religious as well as the political centre of the kingdom which he forthwith established. Like Solomon and Jeroboam I. in later times, he doubtless sought by this means to rally about his throne the religious zeal as well as the patriotism of his followers, and thus insure its stability. Religion, as we have seen, was even at this time a stronger bond than common ancestry. Although it was censured severely by later prophets, Gideon's age regarded this act as most natural and wise. His own tribe of Manasseh was the nucleus of his kingdom; it also included Ephraim to the south and a few towns across the Jordan; its northern boundaries, surely, did not extend far beyond the plain of Esdraelon. Respecting the life of this incipient Hebrew nation under the rule of Gideon, the Bible narrative is silent, unless Judges vi. and vii. contain distant reflections of subsequent conflicts with those desert invaders, the Midianites. It is certain that at this period their power was so completely broken that they never again became a serious menace to the independence of the Hebrews.

6

56. Throughout Israelitish history many of the worst evils that have afflicted the state proceeded from the harem. Because of its baneful influences the first Hebrew kingdom came to ruin three years after the death of its founder. Among his many wives Gideon had taken — perhaps for the purpose of consolidating his kingdom — one of the Canaanitish women of the half-Israelitish town of Shechem. The son by this marriage, Abimelech, after his father's death went to his mother's kinsmen at Shechem, and persuaded them to aid him in seizing the throne. From the temple of Baal-berith (" Baal of the covenant ") they took seventy pieces of silver and gave to the young adventurer. With these he hired kindred spirits, and going to Ophrah ruthlessly slew his seventy brothers. Only one, Jotham, escaped the wholesale murder. Returning to Shechem, Abimelech was crowned king by his kinsmen. The words of truth and warning which Jotham, his brother and the rightful heir of Gideon, uttered as he stood on the heights of Gerazim fell upon deaf ears. The Shechemites, both Hebrews and Canaanites, preferred to put their " trust in the shadow of the bramble." But they profited little by their evil course ; Abimelech made his capital elsewhere, and ruled Shechem through his governor, Zebul. This act soon aroused the dissatisfaction of the Canaanitish element in the city. Certain of them turned highway robbers, and plundered the agents of the king. Finally, the spirit of revolt found a leader in Gaal the son of Ebed, and at the annual harvest feast it blazed into a flame of defiance against their half-Israelitish king. At last the message of his governor brought Abimelech with an army ; an ambuscade drew forth the rebel with

his followers, and they were compelled to flee from the
city. Having tasted blood, Abimelech was merciless
in taking vengeance upon the Shechemites; the people
were slaughtered in great numbers, and under Abimelech's direction the fortress connected with the temple
of El-berith, in which the Canaanites took refuge, was
burned, with its occupants, — in all about one thousand
men and women. The tyranny of Gideon's unworthy
son stirred up repeated revolts among the cities of
Israel. At last in the siege of the citadel of Thebez, a
town east of Shechem, this monster of cruelty met a most
ignominious death, being struck on the head by a mill-
stone thrown by a woman. Thus through the utter
inefficiency and wickedness of Abimelech the first
Hebrew kingdom came to an inglorious end. It clearly
demonstrated the dangers and evils of the kingship;
at the same time it illustrated its advantages. Only
by union under such a permanent organization as the
kingship insured, could the national life and independence of the Israelitish tribes be attained. Later,
therefore, when the need became imperative, the election of a king was not the new and unheard-of experi-
ment that it is often imagined to have been. Already
the idea had taken root during the turbulent period
of the judges.

57. It is impossible to determine with certainty the chronology of events in Hebrew history before the days of David. The ancient narratives contain no chronological data. The notices contained in the books of Judges and Samuel respecting the duration of the rule of the different judges belong to the framework, and are therefore from the hand of the later editor. The prevalence of the number forty, and multiples and fractions thereof, indicates that he was obliged to resort to conjecture, and contented himself with round numbers. It is even difficult to determine the exact relation of the events recorded, except as certain ones lead up to others.

58. The concluding chapter in the history of the period was the subjugation of the Hebrews of the north by the Philistines. The stories which have gathered about the name of Samson indicate that from a very early period an intermittent border-warfare had been carried on between the hill and plain but the ambition of the contestants never suggested more than mutual revenge and reprisal. About the middle of the eleventh century B. C., however, the Philistines began to extend their boundaries. The fertile plain where they had settled as immigrants yielded rich returns for their toils. As they became masters of their land, they reared large, opulent cities,

encircled with the huge walls which are so necessary where Nature has provided no defences. Commerce, which surged up and down the coast plains,
also brought them the products of the art and culture
of that age. Consequently, in civilization and wealth
they were greatly in advance of their neighbors upon
the central plateau of Palestine. Although their political organization crystallized about five distinct cities,
their unity seems to have been far more perfect than
that of the Hebrews. The Danites, who had extended
their settlements out on the plain of Sharon, were
driven back by this advancing power and forced to
seek an abiding place elsewhere.

59. A study of the topography of the western slope
of the central plateau of Palestine explains at once
why the brunt of the Philistine attack fell upon the
northern tribes. The western highlands of Judah are
abrupt and cut by only five or six valleys, which in
places are little more than deep rocky ravines, almost impassable for a large army, and easily defended by a few
men stationed on the overhanging crags ; the mountains of Ephraim on the other hand, especially to the
north, are pierced by a series of broad, shallow valleys
which lead into the heart of the Israelitish territory
and invite the invader. Ephraim also, with its broad
acres and varied products, offered far more tempting
prey than the rugged hills of Judah. Consequently,
when the Philistines rallied their forces for the conquest of the Hebrews, they marched up the coast over the
plain of Sharon to Aphek, which was located probably
at the entrance of the plain of Dothan, which in turn
opens into Esdraelon and commands central Canaan.
Warned of their danger, the Israelitish tribes whose

territory was menaced rallied, and at the entrance of
the hill country met the Philistine army.   The Philistines with their large host and superior equipment
vanquished the Hebrews in the first engagement, and
(according to the old narrative preserved in I. Samuel
iv.) slew four thousand men.   It was the old trouble:
the Israelites were not united, and had no leader to
rally them; Gideon and his deeds were only a memory.   In their extremity, remembering how Jehovah
had delivered them in the battle against the Canaanites beside the Kishon, they caused the Ark to be
brought from Shiloh that Jehovah himself might be
present as their champion.   The Philistines, familiar
with the stories concerning this sacred palladium of
their foes, were at first terrified; but their courage soon
conquered their superstitions.   In the second engagement they gained an overwhelming victory over the
Israelites.   A great number (40,000) of footmen were
slain, and the rest "fled every man to his tent."   Central Canaan was thrown open to the conqueror.

60. Hebrew historians, like those of other peoples,
are frequently silent respecting their national disasters;
but from the scattered references it is clear that the
Philistines followed up their victory.   The destruction
of the sanctuary at Shiloh referred to by Jeremiah
(vii. 12, 14; xxvi. 6) belongs to this period.   Philistine garrisons were established throughout the land of
Israel even as far as Geba in Benjamin (I. Samuel xiii.
3, 4).   The galling yoke of Philistine bondage rested
upon the necks of the conquered Hebrews.   At the
disastrous battle of Aphek the Ark also, about which
gathered those political and religious memories that
were the national pride and inspiration of the tribes,

fell into the hands of the Philistines.   According to
the record, it brought a long series of calamities upon
its captors; each city to which it was transferred was
afflicted by a grievous pestilence.   At last their priests
and diviners were consulted.   Preparing at their advice
five golden tumors and five golden mice as symbols of
the pestilence which had attacked them, they placed
these as a guilt-offering with the Ark upon a new
cart; to the cart they fastened two cows, never yoked
before, and turned them loose at the entrance of the
valley of Sorek which led up toward the land of the
Israelites.   Contrary to brute instincts, the cows left
their calves behind and drew the Ark up the valley
until it rested near the Hebrew town of Beth-shemesh.
To the minds of the Philistines this was conclusive
proof that the dire pestilence was not "a chance that
happened to them," but Jehovah's "hand that smote
them."   Yet even to the Benjaminites who received
the Ark it imparted the same apparently contagious
disease.   Finally, it was placed under the charge of
Eleazar the descendant of Eli, its former guardian at
Shiloh.

61. It is significant that the Ark which bound the
Hebrews to the age and teaching of Moses again
emerged into prominence at this important epoch; but
for the time being it was neglected by them.   According to the naïve, superstitious thought of that age, at
Aphek they had placed their trust in Jehovah and he
had failed them.   As they were ground down under
the hated Philistine bondage, the suspicion began
naturally to creep into the minds of many that the
gods of their masters were superior to their God, or
else that Jehovah had deserted them.   The danger

which threatened the future of the Hebrew cause was again not only a political but a religious one. The period of the judges ends in darkness; but conditions were at last ripe, and in the midst of the general anguish and distress a nation was about to be born.

VI

SOCIAL AND RELIGIOUS CONDITIONS DURING THE PERIOD OF THE JUDGES

62. THE popular conception that the so-called period of the judges was altogether one of retrogression cannot be intelligently maintained. Although the period of childhood of a human being is not the most fruitful either intellectually or spiritually, yet without these years spent in making muscles and sinews, the intellectual and spiritual development of mature years is impossible. Thus it was with the Hebrew people. Without a land, a home, and the growth in culture and ideas which came during this seemingly chaotic epoch, the Hebrews would never have had a message for humanity. It is difficult to measure the progress, first, because it was internal rather than external; and, second, since we are ignorant of just what was the condition of the Hebrew tribes when they emerged from their desert wanderings. We do know that they were nomads with the customs and primitive organization of the modern Arabs. The social unit was the tribe, and the chief wealth and means of subsistence consisted in flocks; but as nomads they had no permanent place of abode, and consequently little culture and almost no history. When they entered Canaan they commenced building permanent homes and establishing towns. They still retained their flocks, but they began also to cultivate the soil. In other words,

they became agriculturists with all that this important transition implies, and the raising of grain and the culture of the vine were their chief occupations. These they learned from the earlier inhabitants, the Canaanites. From the same teachers they also acquired the simple arts which their primitive life made necessary. Among them — as among all peoples in the same stage of civilization — the blacksmith, who manufactured their rude weapons and tools, occupied a position of peculiar honor. The workers in pottery were likewise very essential to their domestic life. Any further needs were supplied directly from the Canaanites, or through the medium of trade. Their wants were necessarily few, since they had at their command but limited means for gratifying them.

63. The life of the early Israelites was that of pioneers, struggling with Nature and adverse circumstances for a livelihood and a home. The repeated waves of foreign invasion often swept away the little that they may have accumulated. Their dwellings were exceedingly rude. A religious people concentrate their building resources upon their sanctuaries; but those of the Hebrews at this time were of the simplest kind, in many cases little more than a circle of stones, ordinarily enclosing a rough altar, canopied by the blue heavens. Yet by degrees, as their numbers rapidly increased by virtue of their more settled mode of living, by extending their boundaries and becoming possessed of the soil, they were laying the foundations for a sturdy national life when once a satisfactory political organization should be evolved.

64. As agriculturists, they began to live together in settled communities for the purpose of society,

trade, and mutual protection. These collections of
homes grew into villages. For refuge in times of invasion a citadel was built, as at Shechem (Judges
ix. 46–49). When the town became populous and
rich, it was encircled by walls. By degrees the primitive patriarchal organization was set aside. Tribal
communism was abandoned as soon as the individuals
in a clan began to acquire fields and houses ; this process began immediately on the entrance into Canaan.
The intermarriage with the Canaanites and Arab
tribes also tended inevitably to weaken the tribal bond.
As communities, often made up of alien elements,
came to live together and in time developed into
villages and cities, the town organization became the
more important, and the family and tribal affinities
were forgotten. Frequent reference is made to the
" men of the town," as for example when Abimelech
attempted to enlist the Shechemites (Judges ix. 2, 6,
23, 26 *et seq.*), — suggesting that most matters of public
interest were decided by a council including all the
free men of a city. The details of the regulation of
the larger towns were in the hands of an oligarchy, —
self-elected, or allowed to rule by common consent
because of their superior ability, or as the representatives of the leading families. These were known as
the " elders " of the town. The east-Jordan village of
Succoth, which was one of moderate size, had seventy-
seven such elders (Judges viii. 14). In keeping with
the manners of the East, the organization was at the
best exceedingly primitive. Chance seemed to rule
and anarchy to be the result; but gradually the germinal
ideas of government were taking root, preparing the
people for the inauguration of the monarchy.

65. The late compiler of the Book of Judges, being a prophet, was principally interested in the religious life of the period; but living in an age when the historic perspective was almost unknown, he unconsciously read into this primitive age the higher religious standards of his own times. The result is that the religious concepts of the sections which are from his hands often present the most striking contrasts with those of the older narratives; yet the evidence of the latter, which is usually the testimony of deeds rather than words, must of course be followed as our guide to a knowledge of the conditions and ideas which actually prevailed. Furthermore, the practices which are accepted without protest by any age are the true indices of its ethical and religious standards. If the actors be the popular heroes of their day, and their action be tacitly commended, the evidence is conclusive.

66. The period of the judges is an admirable illustration of the great principle of spiritual as well as physical development enunciated by the great Teacher, "First the blade, then the ear, then the full corn in the ear" (Mark iv. 28). The seed of divine truth sown by Moses was taking root, and the blade was just beginning to appear. The soil, however, was rocky and filled with thorns; for the Canaanitish civilization, into which they entered and which they in part adopted, was corrupt and tainted with immorality. Murder, provided the victim was a public enemy, was readily condoned. Respecting Ehud, who treacherously slew the king of Moab, the narrative declares that "The Lord raised them up a saviour" (Judges iii. 15). Samson's deeds of wanton destruction were fondly cherished in popular remembrance (Judges xv.

4-8, 15; xvi. 30). Gideon did not hesitate to revenge
the inhospitality of the cowardly elders of Succoth
and Penuel by a wholesale slaughter, even though they
were his kinsmen.   The grim law of blood-revenge
was the statute which the age recognized and rigor-
ously enforced.   The obligation of a vow was regarded
as more binding than the command not to kill.   As
illustration, may be cited the story of Jephthah (Judges
xi. 30, 31) and the vow of King Saul, which nearly
resulted in the death of Jonathan (I. Samuel xiv.).

67. The authority of might was more generally
accepted than that of right.   Foes were barbarously
tortured (Judges i. 6).   Micah, the Ephraimite, did
not hesitate to steal even from his own mother (Judges
xvii. 2).   When the Danites set out to establish a new
colony in the north, they deliberately stole the priest
of Micah with the equipment of his shrine in return
for the wise counsel which their spies had received on
their first expedition.   To Micah's just demand that
they restore his cherished possessions they replied, "Let
not thy voice be heard among us, lest angry fellows fall
upon you, and thou lose thy life, with the lives of thy
household."   The laxity of social morality is indicated
by the acts of such representative men as Gideon and
Samson (Judges viii. 31; xiv. 1, 2; xvi. 1).   Yet the
low practice of the age was due rather to ignorance
than to a deliberate resolve to do wrong; for when the
popular conscience was aroused by some heinous act,
as the crime of the men of Gibeah against the travel-
ling Levite, it gave no uncertain sound.   Through the
mists of barbarism the light of a higher truth was
gradually penetrating; under its fostering influence
the " blade " was slowly developing into the " ear."

68. Since its fruits were so imperfect, we cannot expect to find a very high type of religion prevailing. In external form, at least, there was little to distinguish it from that of the Canaanites in whose territory the Israelites had settled. The Ark was deposited first at Gilgal, and later at Shiloh; but the latter sanctuary soon shared the homage of the Hebrews with many other local shrines situated throughout the land. Among these might be mentioned Beersheba, Tabor, Ramah, Mizpah, and Penuel; many of these were originally held sacred by the Canaanites, and were in turn adopted by the Israelites. Bethel ("House of El"), as its name indicates, had long been a sacred town among the old inhabitants. The name Gilgal means a "circle;" and the many towns thus designated, scattered throughout the land of Canaan, recall the ancient Baal worship. At Shechem, as has already been noted, the Israelites and Canaanites had so far united the worship of Jehovah and Baal that they shared a common sanctuary, which they called the temple of Baal-berith, or El-berith ("Lord of the covenant"). Since the term *Baal* means "Lord" or "Master," it was very easy for the Hebrews to apply it to their national God; that they did so is further indicated by the recurrence of names containing the ending *baal*, — as for example Jerubbaal, Ishbaal (the son of Saul), and Meribaal (the son of Jonathan). The northern Israelitish prophet, Hosea, clearly states that the practice of calling Jehovah *Baal* had continued even down to his day (Hosea ii. 16).

69. In addition to the public sanctuaries, private families had their own religious establishments. The history of that of Micah, the Ephraimite, preserved in

Judges xvii. is most instructive. The eleven hundred
pieces of silver which he had stolen from his mother
and subsequently returned were dedicated by her to
Jehovah; she accordingly gave them to her son in
order that he might make a "graven image and a
molten image." With two hundred of the silver
pieces the founder made an image which was set up in
Micah's house; the other accessories of an early Hebrew temple — the ephod and the teraphim, the family
gods — were also secured. At first one of Micah's
sons was set apart to be the priest at this family sanctuary. Later, however, a Levite of Bethlehem of
Judah, a descendant of Moses, came northward seeking
a home; by offering ten pieces of silver annually and
his food and clothing, Micah persuaded him to remain,
and forthwith consecrated him to be his priest. This
sanctuary, so auspiciously established, soon gained such
prestige that its oracle was consulted by the Danites
when they were seeking a new home. Reference has
already been made to their subsequent capture of the
priest, ephod, teraphim, image, and all. The Levite
was persuaded by the prospect of a greater following
to connive with his captors. At their new home at the
foot of Mount Hermon the Danites established a religious shrine, which later emerges into prominence as
one of the two royal sanctuaries of Jeroboam I. Similarly, Gideon in founding his kingdom made an image
from the spoils taken from the Midianites, and set it up
in his new capital at Ophrah.

70. In adopting the sacred places of the Canaanites,
the Hebrews undoubtedly accepted many of their religious customs in addition to those already shared in
common as the universal heritage of the Semitic world.

Besides the sacrifice of animals, that of human beings was not unknown, as the fate of Jephthah's daughter indicates. Unfortunately, the practice did not disappear completely during this period, but was revived again by the Judean king, Ahaz (II. Kings xvi. 3). Each Israelite was allowed to offer sacrifice, although a tendency was beginning to manifest itself to delegate this religious service to certain ones especially set apart for the office; already the Levite, or at least the descendant of Moses, was regarded as especially eligible. It is difficult to generalize respecting the religious customs throughout all Israel during this turbulent period, since undoubtedly they varied greatly in different parts of the land. Where the Canaanitish influence was strong, the external fusion at least between the two religions was almost complete. In those regions where the simpler pastoral life was preserved, the purer worship of the desert prevailed. This was especially true in the south, where the assimilation was with Arabian rather than Canaanitish tribes.

71. To understand the religious history of this formative, transition period, it is necessary constantly to remember that Israel's religious and political life was inseparably connected. The idea of Jehovah's unity was in part commensurate with Israel's unity; therefore when disunited, the Hebrews were peculiarly susceptible to the temptations of the Canaanitish cult with its many local deities. Whenever they were led by stress of circumstances to unite against a common foe, their loyalty to Jehovah was intensified; consequently, the repeated waves of foreign invasion which swept over them in the end proved their salvation, for it aroused them from their lethargy and led them to

turn to Jehovah for deliverance. In a broad sense, therefore, the late editor of the Book of Judges presents the true religious philosophy of the age. With many of the historic details he was unfamiliar, but as an enlightened prophet he had caught the great truth that a loving God was leading his people onward, even through darkness, by means of the varied and trying experiences of their history.

72. The conceptions of Jehovah's character were as simple and undeveloped as the age. Jephthah voiced the idea of his contemporaries when he declared to the invading Ammonites: "Jehovah, the God of Israel, hath dispossessed the Amorites from before his people Israel, and shouldst thou possess them? Wilt thou not possess that which Chemosh thy god giveth thee to possess? So whatsoever Jehovah our God hath dispossessed from before us, them will we possess" (Judges xi. 23, 24). Centuries passed before enlightened prophets proclaimed for the first time that "the gods of the other nations were no gods." The early Hebrews conceived of Chemosh as the god of the Moabites, just as Jehovah was their God. The essential tenet in their faith was that Jehovah was the *one* God who commanded their allegiance as a nation. The ignorant masses frequently forgot even this, and also worshipped the Canaanitish Baalim. Yet they never ceased to regard Jehovah as the God of their race; in times of national danger they "came up to the help of the Lord against the mighty;" to him they turned for deliverance in the hour of distress, and he gave them victory; in fact, in everything that befell them they recognized his hand. It is significant, also, that before the close of the period the land of the Hebrews is con-

ceived of as Jehovah's land. The God of Sinai and of the wandering had become the God of Canaan. Worship at the many local shrines is sufficient evidence that the people believed that the unseen God whom they still endeavored symbolically to represent by images was present in the new abode of his people. The important and dangerous transition from the life of the desert to that of Canaan was safely made, and the national trust and confidence in Jehovah was deepened rather than lost. Foreign cults were destined from time to time to contest with the religion of Jehovah, the service of the Hebrews; but Jehovah was from henceforth the one God of the Israelitish people.

PART III

HISTORY OF THE UNITED KINGDOM

I

HISTORICAL SOURCES

73. THE Book of I. Samuel, which is the historical
source for the reign of Saul, claims to be and clearly is
a compilation of material gleaned from earlier sources
and arranged by a later editor. Chronological sequence
receives much more attention here than in the Book
of Judges, although in many cases the work of compilation is evident. In chapters viii.–xiv. the chief
characters are Saul and Samuel. As in the accounts
of Gideon in the Book of Judges, two distinct strands
of narrative are woven together. The extracts from
the oldest sources are found in chapters ix. 1–x. 16,
xi., xiii. 1–7^{a}; xiii. 15^{b}–xiv. 46, and form a connected
unit in themselves. Their style and ideas are those of
the ancient records in Judges ; their historical representation is in perfect, keeping with preceding and
subsequent conditions in Israel ; they are the unit
which consistently binds the past with the future.
Consequently, in them we recognize our true source
for information respecting the facts and forces which
characterize this important epoch.

74. While the historic testimony of the remaining
portions of this section is quite different from that of
the oldest narratives, it is consistent with itself, — suggesting that they also constitute an independent unit.
In language and ideas they are related to the so-called

Deuteronomic sections of Judges and I. Samuel vii.
2–17 (sect. 34).   Chapter xii., for example, reiterates
the familiar formula, — apostasy, oppression, penitence,
and deliverance.   All Israel are conceived of as acting
in conjunction.   The writer evidently is so far removed
from the events that he has completely forgotten that
their Philistine masters were present to prevent any public convocation for the election of a king.   Sharing the
idea of the later editor of Judges, that the judges followed one another in regular succession, he represents
Samuel as following Eli in the judgeship of all Israel,
and his sons as succeeding him.   But according to the
older narratives (chapters ix. and x. 1–16) Samuel was
only a seer of southwestern Ephraim, who enjoyed a
local reputation for faithfully predicting the future; he
apparently was unknown to such a well-informed man as
Saul.   The great work of the Ephraimite seer was the
selection of a king to deliver the Israelites from their
bondage; but the Samuel of the later writings is represented as bitterly opposing the institution.   The language in which he condemns it (chapter viii.) is almost
a literal description of the abuses of the royal preroga-
tive under such kings as Solomon and Ahab.

75. It is not difficult to see why the later prophets
regarded the kingship as a mistake.   Anything good
in itself, if abused, becomes an evil.   Later kings certainly did misuse their opportunities, and introduced
that Orientalism which was such a deadly menace to
the pure worship of Jehovah (sect. 149).   Furthermore, the souls of these same later prophets were fired
with a far higher ideal.   In the age of Samuel the
kingship represented a great step forward, for thereby
the Hebrews emerged from anarchy into a state of

order. With most nations the next step was from monarchy to democracy; but even democracy, under which individuals are bound together for the attainment of their own personal ends, has its evils and abuses. The later Hebrew prophets realized that there was something higher. This was a type of organization in which all recognized as the uniting bond the love for a common Father, which in turn inspired a mutual love and interest for one another. In a word, these later prophets (as their other writings demonstrate) had not only seen objectively illustrated the evils of the kingship, but they had also caught glimpses of that ideal theocracy which in the light of the teaching of the prophets and of Jesus we know as the Kingdom of God in which the supreme authority is the will of the Highest. Not having the historical spirit, in writing of the times of the judges they naturally projected their ideal into this formative period. Similarly, they conceived of Samuel as not only creating the monarchy, but (like the later prophets) personally directing its policy, or in bitter opposition when his commands as the ambassador of Jehovah were disobeyed. The old records demonstrate that as a matter of fact the order of the prophets was, like the Hebrew nation at that time, only in its infancy.

76. Just how far these later sections have certain historical facts at their basis is a difficult question to answer. Each individual case must be studied in detail by itself. For example, in chapter xiii. 7[b]–15[a] and chapter xv., two independent accounts are given of the rejection of Saul by Samuel. Each is ignorant of the testimony of the other, and it is difficult to reconcile them satisfactorily. Both, in view of their lan-

guage, thought, and representation, are evidently later
than the older thread of narrative; but of the two,
chapter xv., whose background is the Amalekite war
recorded in chapter xiv. 48, is most in harmony with
the ancient sources and conditions.

77. From the fifteenth chapter through the book of
I. Samuel the interest of the authorities cited is with
David. Saul is regarded more unfavorably than in
the opening chapters. The language and representation of chapter xvi. 1–13 proclaim its affinity with
the later stratum of narrative contained in viii., xii.,
and xv. The remainder of the chapter, however, is
old. This records the introduction of the youthful
David, already "a mighty man of valor, and a man of
war and prudent in speech" (xvi. 18), to the court of
Saul, and of his winning the favor of the king until the
latter makes him his armor-bearer. If we had not discovered that the Book of Samuel is a compilation, we
should share with the translators of the Septuagint the
difficulty which led them to leave out a large part of
the following chapter in the fruitless endeavor to reconcile it with the preceding. For chapter xvii. 1–
xviii. 5 tells of the victory of the lad David over
Goliath, and of his subsequent introduction to Saul
and his court, who are wholly unacquainted with the
youthful champion. Even if this section be placed before xvi. 14–23, the difficulty is not entirely removed.
It is further increased when we read in II. Samuel
xxi. 19, "And there was again war with the Philistines at Gob; and Elhanan, the son of Jaare-oregim
the Bethlehemite, slew Goliath the Gittite, the staff of
whose spear was like a weaver's beam" (cf. I. Sam.
xvii. 7). Evidently, here are distinct narratives handed

down through different channels. Whether the Goliath mentioned was actually slain by David or Elhanan can never be absolutely determined. The statement of I. Chronicles xx. 5, that it was a brother of Goliath who fell by the hand of Elhanan, seems to be an endeavor of the later chronicler to harmonize the two statements in Samuel. It is by no means impossible, however, that in some one of the many forays of the Philistines into Judah the youthful David slew the champion of the Philistines. The memory of the act was preserved among David's kinsmen, the Judeans, until at last it found a place in the prophetic history which is our great source for the period. Certainly, some such deed or deeds he performed before he gained the reputation of being "a mighty man of valor," which he bore when introduced to Saul's court. His subsequent record confirms this conclusion.

78. Chapters xviii.–xx. are so lacking in unity that it is impossible to reconcile perfectly the testimony of their different sections; they are compiled from the older and later records of David's deeds, with several insertions from subsequent editors. The testimony of the Septuagint version respecting chapter xviii. 6–30 is valuable; it omits those verses which are in the spirit of the later David-narratives, preserving the older material, which continues the thought of chapter xvi. 14–23. The Septuagint reads — 6^b–8^a, 12^a, 13–16, 20, 21^a, 22–26^a, 27–29^a. Accepting this text, certain inconsistencies are removed. Section xix. 1–17 appears to be based upon the later David-stories, while in xix. 18–24 we at once recognize the language and representation of a late prophetic writer. The latter passage also contains a duplicate account of the origin of the pro-

verb, "Is Saul also among the prophets?" which presents such variations in time and circumstance from its parallel in chapter x. 11–13 that both can hardly be accepted as historical. The claims of the other passage to antiquity and authenticity are so strong that they in turn confirm the conjectures that section xix. 18–24 is among the latest in the book, being related to chapters vii., viii., xii. The connection between chapter xx. and the preceding is not close; but the character of the material is such as to suggest that the information was gleaned from old and reliable sources, and then worked over by a later editor.

79. The remainder of the book for the most part belongs to the original David-narrative. In a few places the work of the editor is apparent. It is probable that the account of David's flight to Achish, king of Gath, in chapter xxi. 10–15, is a later insertion, for it is entirely out of harmony with the context and with David's reputation for prudence; its origin is to be found in his subsequent action in going over to the Philistines. Chapters xxiii. 14, xxiv. 22, and xxvi. contain two accounts of the pursuit of David by Saul, and of the magnanimity of the outlaw in sparing the life of "the Lord's anointed." Although the geographical setting is different, yet the similarity in phraseology and thought is so striking that they may well be regarded as duplicate versions of the same incident. The earlier and simpler is found in chapter xxvi. Section xxviii. 3–25, which records Saul's visit to the witch of Endor, was evidently inserted between chapter xxviii. 2 and xxix. 1, which are closely connected. According to xxix. 1, the Philistines were still at Aphek, south of the plain of Esdraelon, while

in xxviii. 3–25 they are represented as already encamped at Shunem. This passage, therefore, properly
belongs between chapters xxx. and xxxi., immediately
before the account of the battle of Gilboa. Although
its antiquity has been questioned, if we except verses
17 and 18, which were seemingly introduced to con-
nect this section with the late prophetic passages, it
is in representation and language in entire harmony
with the situation and with the character of Saul as set
forth in the old records.

80. The older David-narratives are also the main
sources for II. Samuel. Here the work of the later
editor is not as marked as in I. Samuel. The material
in the opening chapters is systematically arranged; it
corresponds to that of the Samuel-history in the preceding book. Chapters i.–vii. record the successive steps
by which David came to the throne of all Israel, his
capture of Jerusalem and the transference thither of
the Ark. Chapter viii. epitomizes his public acts,
bringing his history to a close, and anticipating events
which are presented in greater detail in the succeeding
section; although its sources were old, this chapter
in its present form is probably from the later editor.
According to i. 5–16, the messenger who avowed that
he himself slew Saul, paid, at David's command, the
penalty for the deed with his own life. This story was
probably gleaned by the editor from some later David-
narrative, for the context is complete without it. In
I. Samuel xxxi. 5, it is definitely stated that Saul fell
by his own hand. The words of David in II. Samuel
iv. 10 — " When one told me, saying, Behold, Saul is
dead, thinking to have brought good tidings, I took
hold of him, and slew him in Ziklag, which was the

reward I gave him for his tidings " — indicate clearly
that David was ignorant of the events recorded in the
passage in question. The chronological notices in ii.
10ᵃ, 11, are also later insertions, for they only interrupt
the sequence of the thought of the old narrative; the
same is true of section iii. 2–5, which seems to have
been detached from the other records of David's family
history, preserved in chapters ix.-xx. The reference to
the early history of Jonathan's son in iv. 4 is likewise
irrelevantly introduced into the midst of the account
of the assassination of Saul's successor by the two
treacherous Benjaminites. The chronological data in
v. 4–5 are also from the later editor. It is probable
that David desired to rear a temple to Jehovah, but
the language and religious spirit of chapter vii. is
plainly Deuteronomic ; it belongs, therefore, in the
same class with the later sections in Judges and
I. Samuel (sect. 34).

81. The second main division of the book (chapters ix.-xx.) recounts in greater detail the events of
David's private and court life. There is evidence that
they are not from the same hand as the other David-
narratives, yet they also are manifestly old; they are
likewise characterized by their freedom from later insertions. Evidently, the final editor incorporated them
almost *in toto* in the present book, preserving them in
the form in which he found them. The remaining
chapters (xxi.-xxiv.) constitute an appendix, which
was probably added to the body of the book after that
had assumed its present form. The appendix consists
of extracts from old records which treated of the reign
of David ; these are loosely bound together. The two
sections — xxi. 1–14 and xxiv. 1–25 — are closely re-

lated; it is more than possible that originally they
immediately followed each other, but have been separated by the insertion of the intervening material.
Another striking example of a later insertion is found
between xxi. 15–22 and xxiii. 8–39; both of these passages, in an annalistic style, record the names and
deeds of David's heroes. The poetical material thus
introduced (xxii. 1–xxiii. 7) is assigned to David; but,
like Hannah's song of I. Samuel, its language and
thought suggest a period much later than that of the
united kingdom.

82. The history of David is concluded and that of
Solomon is introduced in I. Kings i. and ii. These
chapters are closely related to the extracts from David's
family history, preserved in II. Samuel ix.–xx. Like
the latter, they contain few traces of editorial revision.
The language of ii. 2–4 is that which is characteristic
of a much later age. The chronological notices, ii. 10,
11, are also probably from the editor. Subsequent
events in Solomon's reign are recorded in chapters
iii.–xi.; his wisdom, might, and splendor are first presented. These are but the introduction to the great
event of his age, — at least in the eyes of subsequent
generations, — the building of the Temple. The history is concluded in chapter xi., with a review of his
reign, in which the author (a later prophet) points out
the evils of Solomon's policy. The arrangement and
character of the material suggest that the historical
data were collected from earlier sources, and recast in
the present form in the spirit and according to the
methods of the modern historian. The "Book of the
Acts of Solomon" was at least one of the sources from
which the editor gathered his facts. These chronicles

were probably based upon state annals, or an official
record of events. Their testimony is of the highest
value, because they practically represent contemporary
history. Where these were silent, prophetical narratives, or else current traditions respecting the wisdom
and glory of Solomon, were incorporated. In certain
cases the numbers have grown during the period of
oral transmission, as for example in v. 15, 16. Such
a history as this seems to have taken form before the
days of Josiah. In common with the other early narratives, it received certain additions from the Deuteronomic editors. The latest insertions were from the
final editor of the books of Kings, who lived during
the Babylonian exile.

83. Without going into detail, the material may be
classified under these different heads. Chapters iii.
4–13 and 16–28 are based upon early prophetical narratives, while verses 2, 3, 14, and 15 were clearly
inserted by a later editor, who read his ideas and
phraseology into the older records. The source of iv.
1–19, 27–28, may well have been the "Book of the
Acts of Solomon." In the Septuagint text, verse 27
immediately follows verse 19. The intermediate verses,
20–26, were written by an editor living in the exile.
Section iv. 29–v. 18 is founded upon relatively old
sources, possibly the state annals. The same is true of
chapters vi. and vii., which describe the building enterprises of Solomon. It is not improbable that part of
the information therein presented was preserved in the
Temple archives. The unmistakable phraseology of vi.
11–13 betrays its Deuteronomic origin. Chapters viii.
1–ix. 9 also abound in indications of late authorship.
Section viii. 1–22, however, rests upon a historical

foundation; the language and thought of the remainder of the passage is strongly Deuteronomic. Chapters ix. 10–x. 29 consist of a series of notices concerning Solomon's foreign and home policy; they are loosely bound together, and in some cases present variations from the testimony of the preceding sections, which suggest that the editor collected his data from a variety of sources. The original substratum in chapter xi. was an account of the adversaries who opposed Solomon's rule, — Hadad the Edomite, Rezon the Syrian, and Jeroboam the Ephraimite; possibly it also contained reference to his many wives, and the pernicious influence of the various religions which they brought with them. The Deuteronomic editor has not only worked over this early material, but has also presented his estimate of the sins of Solomon. This religious philosophy of history is most apparent in verses 2, 9–13, 33–39. The concluding verses, 41–43, are the regular formula of the final editor of the Book of Kings.

84. In this hasty analysis of the books of Samuel and Kings, it has been impossible either to go into details or to indicate the cumulative evidence upon which the conclusions presented are based; for these the student is referred to the text itself, and the various authorities who have treated it exhaustively. (See Appendix.) The present study, however, is sufficient to indicate the general character of the sources and their respective value to the Hebrew historian. Since the books of Chronicles were not written until after the return from the Babylonian exile, and are chiefly dependent upon the older records of Samuel and Kings for their data respecting this early period, they contribute little additional information. Whatever be the

date of the Song of Songs, its historical value is great, since it presents the impression which Solomon's character and policy made upon his own and subsequent generations; it also confirms and amplifies the testimony of the oldest prophetic records.

II

STEPS LEADING TO THE ESTABLISHMENT OF THE HEBREW KINGDOM

85. AT last, after many long, weary years, Israel was about to be delivered from its bondage in Canaan. The preceding period of anarchy had taught the Hebrews by bitter experiences certain invaluable lessons. Repeatedly it had been impressed upon them that by union alone could they maintain their freedom in the midst of the aggressive, hostile nations which encircled them. The only type of permanent organization of which their age and stage of civilization was cognizant was the kingship. Local deliverers did not suffice, for the relief which they afforded was only temporary. At this time also not one blow, but many, strong and united, must be struck before the iron fetters of Philistine bondage could be broken. The very existence of the Israelites as a distinct race, and consequently the future of Jehovah's religion, imperatively demanded a king. The idea was not foreign to their thought. The kingship was a long-established institution among the neighboring peoples, whom they regarded as their kinsmen, and through the ill-starred kingdom of Gideon they had been personally introduced to it. Its evils, therefore, were fresher in the minds of the Hebrews of central Israel than its advantages. There is every reason for accepting the testi-

8

mony of the oldest narrative in Samuel, and believing that the first steps toward its institution were taken, not by the people who had given themselves up to despair, but by a Jehovah-enlightened seer, who, like Moses and Deborah before him, grasping the situation and appreciating what must be done, proceeded to act.

86. There is also ground for concluding that Samuel was not entirely without support. At this critical period bands of prophets appeared for the first time in Israelitish history. It is clear that these so-called "sons of the prophets" should not be classed with such enlightened national teachers as Amos or Isaiah. In fact, Amos emphatically declared that he was not one of the "sons of the prophets" (Amos vii. 14). At this early formative period these bands gathered about the sanctuaries, kindling their religious zeal with the aid of the wild, weird music which an ancient Oriental drew forth from the psaltery, timbrel, pipe, and harp (I. Sam. x. 5). This threw them into a state of ecstasy very analogous to that which may be observed to-day among the Mohammedan dervishes, or in the revival services so popular with certain colored people of the South. With greater light these practices disappeared from among the Hebrews, and the "sons of the prophets" fell into ill repute. The religious ideas of one age often seem mere superstitions to the succeeding, to which has been revealed something higher and better. Certain of their own contemporaries evidently regarded these enthusiasts a little contemptuously, deeming them mere fanatics (I. Sam. x. 11–13); but because the expression of their religious zeal was not of the highest type, its true significance should not be overlooked. It

has been suggested that they were aroused to activity
by the shame of the Philistine dominance. Certainly
the object of their zeal was Jehovah and his worship,
and this would inevitably arouse a burning patriotism
and a longing again "to come up to the help of Jehovah against the mighty." The flame which kindled
the conflagration that drove away the Philistines was
loyalty to Jehovah. It is, therefore, exceedingly suggestive that after leaving Samuel, and before he struck
the blow which led to his election to the kingship, Saul
came into contact with these politico-religious fanatics,
and catching their spirit was so transformed that his
associates and kinsmen noted it (I. Sam. x. 10–16).
The old narratives indicate that Samuel was familiar
and in touch with these prophetic bands (chapters ix.
and x.) ; a later record places him at the head of one
of their guilds, which was located at his home in
Ramah (I. Sam. xix. 18–24). These chance references warrant the conclusion that Samuel did not
stand alone, but enjoyed the sympathy and support
of the various prophetic bands scattered throughout
the land. The latter were an index of the need and
the spirit of the time. In turn they must have aided
in arousing the dormant patriotism of their more phleg-
matic countrymen.

87. Subsequent writers undoubtedly conceived of
Samuel according to their own ideals ; but the tendency to exalt his memory can be explained only by a
historical Samuel, who impressed his strong personality
upon his own and following generations. The Samuel of the earliest records and his work are none the
less grand because so simple. He went about his important mission, not as the regularly elected judge and

religious head of all Israel, but as a seer who had won
the respect of the more earnest and religious in central
Israel. Although Saul, the warrior, had not heard of
him, his reputation was known to the servant of Kish.
When the future champion of Israel returned, his uncle
eagerly asked, " Tell me, I pray thee, what Samuel
said unto you." The narrative is late which introduces
us to the boyhood days of Samuel at the old sanctuary
at Shiloh, yet it probably has a historic foundation.
Such an experience would alike fit him for his great
life-work, and give him a prestige shared by no other
priest or seer.

88. Shiloh was in ruins, the ark almost forgotten,
and the priests scattered. The Hebrews acknowledged
little authority other than that of their Philistine masters ; but that little was exercised by those who were
recognized as Jehovah's representatives. Above all,
the needs of the situation gave unlimited power to the
man who could point out a way of deliverance. Probably Samuel, in common with many of the more enlightened patriots of Israel, had long been looking for
a man possessed of courage and energy, and who at the
same time could unite and command others. At last
the right one was found ; a seeming chance brought
him to Samuel's doors. The asses of a certain Kish, a
prominent Benjaminite, had wandered from home ; his
son Saul, pleasing in manner, and head and shoulders
above his fellows, was dispatched with a servant to
seek for them. They proceed in their search through
northern Benjamin, up among the hills of Ephraim ;
but in vain. When they reach the district known as
Zuph, Saul proposes that they return, lest their long
absence cause alarm at home ; the servant, however,

urges him to consult a certain seer living in a town not far away, who was held in high honor and enjoyed a reputation for predicting the future with certainty. Accordingly, taking a small piece of silver as the fee, they set out to visit this man of God. As they go up the ascent to the town, — whose name, Ramah, indicates that it was one of those many cities in Israel perched upon a hill, — they meet certain maidens of the village; from them they learn that the townsmen on that day are sacrificing in the high place, and that the seer is present to bless their sacrifice. At the entrance of the town Samuel meets them. His enlightened vision had enabled him to recognize the man for the crisis. One of the neutral tribe of Benjamin would be most likely to unite the rival factions of the north and south. Saul possessed a commanding figure, which in his age was the first requisite in one who was to lead men; he furthermore was courageous, energetic, and patriotic. As the seer receives the Benjaminite prince and invites him to partake of the banquet which he has had prepared in his honor, his words indicate that he was intimately acquainted with Saul, even though Saul did not know him; for he added, " And I will tell thee all that is in thine heart." Samuel's suggestions were destined to fall into good soil, for it is evident that already Israel's future king was meditating upon the people's wrongs, and questioning whether or not he was called to act.

89. Assuring him that the asses for which he was searching had been found, the venerable seer, in a characteristically Oriental manner, proceeds to the important business in hand. The words in which Samuel introduces his guest at the banquet indicate that others

in Israel were also beginning to regard this young Benjaminite as a possible deliverer : " On whom is all the
desire of Israel? Is it not on thee, and on all thy
father's house ? " Saul's reply shows that modesty
also was one of his virtues. Samuel moves straight
on toward the accomplishment of his purpose. At the
village feast he significantly assigns the place of honor
to his guest, and causes the choicest portion to be set
before him; at night he entertains and " communes
with Saul upon the housetop." The most important
symbolic act was reserved for the morrow. When
they are about to part at the lower end of the town,
the seer solemnly anoints Saul, in the name of Jehovah, — thus publicly proclaiming his call to the kingship. Samuel also makes certain predictions, which,
as they come to pass, are to establish in Saul's mind
the truth of his prophetic message. He, however,
makes no announcement as to when or how Saul is
to be raised to the kingship; he simply sends him
forth with the suggestive advice, " Do thyself as thine
hand shall find, for God is with thee."

90. Saul departed, his soul filled with a mighty resolve. In the graphic language of the old record, " God
turned him another heart." To the astonishment of
his acquaintances he affiliated with the religio-patriotic
bands of the prophets, and was even found prophesy-
ing among them; their amazement found expression in
the popular proverb, " Is Saul also among the prophets ? " But the occasion was not yet ripe, and therefore,
in answering his uncle's curious questions concerning
what Samuel had said to him, he made no mention of
the words which had fired his soul. Quietly he resumed
his accustomed tasks; but erelong his ready hand

"found something to do." The Ammonites, under
their king Nahash, taking advantage of the weakness
of the Israelites, advanced against the east-Jordan town
of Jabesh-gilead, and not only demanded its surrender,
but threatened to put out the right eyes of its inhabitants, as a reproach to Israel. Messengers from the
fated town passed throughout all the land, beseeching
aid from their kinsmen. The sacred law of blood-
revenge commanded them to heed the cry, but no one
responded until the messengers came to Gibeah; here
the men of the town "lifted up their voices and wept."
Saul, coming from the field with his oxen, inquired,
"What aileth the people that they weep?" When
he learned the cause, "the spirit of the Lord came
mightily upon Saul." His patriotic resolve took form
in action. Without hesitating a moment, he cut up a
yoke of oxen and sent these bloody reminders of duty
throughout Israel, with the threat that the oxen of
those who did not respond would meet a similar fate.
At last the Hebrews recognized that there was one
among them whom they could regard as their leader.
In great numbers they rallied about his standard;
north and south were both represented. Marching to
the relief of the beleaguered town, Saul divided his
forces into three companies, and surprised the Ammonites in an early morning attack; the foe was routed
and scattered. By this victory the city of Jabesh-
gilead was rescued, the Israelites gained a new confidence, and, above all, the cause of national freedom
found a leader. When they returned to Gilgal the
Hebrews hastened, as in the days of Gideon, to make
him their king who had already evinced his ability to
command. The seed sown by Samuel had begun to

bear fruit. It is not improbable that the seer also improved the opportunity to instruct the infant nation respecting Jehovah's will in the spirit if not in the language of the later narrative, preserved in chapter xii. The date of this simple but portentous act is to be found somewhere (about 1037) during the latter part of the eleventh century before the Christian era.

91. In accepting the kingship, Saul entered upon a heritage of war. His title was an empty one until he had won a kingdom. The Philistine masters of the land could not reasonably object to the expedition for the relief of Jabesh-gilead; but when their Hebrew subjects elected their victorious leader king, it was virtually a declaration of war. Jonathan, Saul's son, left no room for doubt by attacking the Philistine garrison at Geba immediately upon the return of the Hebrews from across the Jordan. With their characteristic activity the Philistines at once poured a huge army into the land of the Hebrews, overrunning it as far as Michmash, on the southern borders of the mountains of Ephraim; by this strategic movement connection was severed between Saul and the strong tribes of the north. For a generation or more the Hebrews had been accustomed only to defeat. In the presence of the Philistines Saul's army vanished. Many "hid themselves in caves and in thickets, and in rocks and in holes, and in cisterns," and some even fled across the Jordan; others submitted to the Philistines without striking a blow for freedom. The handful of six hundred men who remained with Saul "followed him trembling." The inauguration of the Hebrew kingdom was not altogether glorious.

92. Meeting with no resistance, and evidently not

desiring at once to invade the more rocky territory to the south, the Philistine army divided into three parts and turned back to pillage. At this critical moment, when the Hebrew cause seemed lost, Jonathan, who had been placed in charge of the stronghold of Geba, turned the tide of battle by a deed of personal daring. The deep valley of Michmash, which leads up from the Jordan, separated the fortress of Geba from that of Michmash to the north, where a garrison of Philistines had been left to watch the Hebrews and guard the rear of their army. Down the face of the precipice climbed the undaunted Jonathan with his armor-bearer; he crossed the narrow ravine and began to mount up among the steep rocks toward the heights above, which were held by the Philistines. The latter regarded these two men with utter contempt: "Behold the Hebrews come forth out of the holes where they had hid themselves!" In silence and unmolested the two advanced. The contempt and wonder of the Philistines were soon changed to alarm as the intrepid prince fell upon them single-handed and began to slay them. Fear lest it was an ambuscade, or superstition lest it was a god who had attacked them, quickly seized the foe. This terror, which the Hebrew historian styles "a trembling of God," spread to the plundering bands, who were, as the experience of even modern warfare demonstrates, most susceptible to a panic. The rout was so general that the watchmen of Saul at Gibeah in Benjamin perceived it. The absence of Jonathan and his armor-bearer suggested the cause. At first Saul, still in doubt, started to consult the oracle through the priest; but before the ceremony was completed he rallied the Hebrews for the attack. In the confusion the Philistines fought against each other; the Israelites in their ranks turned against them, and those in hiding came forth to share the victory. Saul, with his characteristic impetuosity, rashly placed a curse upon the head of the one eating food before nightfall. The Hebrews hunted the Philistines out of central Canaan; but the blow was not what it might have been, because they were weakened by lack of food. Saul's rash curse would have cost also the life of the hero of the day, had it not been for the intercession of the people.

III

93. THE first victory over the Philistines was by no means final. These stalwart, brave foes of the Israelites soon reassembled their forces, and again poured up from the plain into the valleys of Ephraim. But their first success gave the Hebrews courage, and taught them that their old masters were not invincible. Saul's reign was one long intermittent war, and his court was perforce a military camp. In the intervals between the Philistine wars he struck blows on other sides, against foes which menaced the independence of the Hebrews. Unfortunately, the old records are silent respecting the details of these wars.

94. According to a later narrative, preserved in chapter xv., it was in one of these expeditions conducted against the Amalekites, those desert robbers who were constantly invading the territory of the Judeans, that Saul incurred the displeasure of Samuel. The king's sin, as therein portrayed, was his failure to slay all his captives in accordance with the prophet's command; a still later section (xiii. 7ᵇ–15ᵃ) attributes Saul's rejection by Samuel to ritualistic reasons. From neither of these accounts is it possible to ascertain the real cause; but their existence gives ground for believing that an alienation in time arose between the seer, representing the intensely religious

party, and Saul, the leader of Israel's armies. Its exact nature perhaps may never be determined; but there is enough in the character of the two men, as revealed in the old records and in the light of the situation, to suggest wherein they must have differed. Before Saul was elected king there were two parties in Israel. One was the religio-patriotic party, which naturally included the religious zealots found in the prophetic bands, enlightened seers like Samuel, the priests, and the more pious among the Israelites. In their minds Jehovah's interests and those of their race were synonymous; if the two seemed to conflict, they would unhesitatingly place those of Jehovah first. On their platform, as it was further developed, stood the later prophets. The other may be styled the political party. It included the nobles of Israel, the military class, and the less stable in the community, who were ready to gain their ends by fair means or foul. The movement toward national independence came from the religio-patriotic party. Saul, because of his personal ability, was called by them to lead it. The old proverb, "Is Saul among the prophets?" hints at the trouble. Impulsive, headstrong, superstitious rather than genuinely religious, he did not feel at home "among the prophets;" their demands seemed too high for their age. The principles which would appeal most strongly to Saul were those of the political party; to them he listened more and more. At a later period, in a fit of jealousy, he ordered the execution of all the priests of Nob. By this act he forever alienated the class in Israel which had called him to the throne.

95. The feeling that he was gradually estranging the best and most intensely loyal elements in his king-

dom probably contributed toward the embittering of Saul's soul. He was the one to lead a sudden attack or inspire courage; but his position called for cool judgment, executive ability, and perseverance. In these qualities he was deficient; consequently, he began to realize that he was losing his grasp of the situation. On the other hand, the harassing border-warfare with the Philistines constantly irritated and vexed Israel's king, until at times a deep melancholia settled down upon him. In the naïve thought of the age, his contemporaries declared that "the spirit of the Lord [the old patriotic enthusiasm] had departed from Saul, and an evil spirit from the Lord troubled him."

96. It was to drive away this evil spirit that David, Israel's future king, was introduced to the military court of Saul. Already this son of Jesse, the Bethle-hemite, in addition to his renown as a cunning player on the harp, enjoyed the reputation of being "a mighty man of valor and a man of war, and skilful in busi-ness, and a comely person." The success which had attended all that he attempted had led public opinion to declare "the Lord is with him." David was one of those peculiarly favored beings who quickly win the favor of all with whom they come in contact. In com-mon with others, "Saul loved him greatly." When dark moods seized the monarch, the Judean harpist was able to dispel them. His skill with the sword soon se-cured for him also the high office of king's armor-bearer. In Saul's service he had ample opportunity to show his powers. From the wars with the Philistines he came back covered with glory. People and court were won by his grace; his warlike renown began to rival that of Israel's king. To have remained at the head

of the Hebrew state at this time a man must have been the chief among his subjects. In David's sudden leap into popularity there was perhaps a menace to the stability of Saul's throne. The king's strained relations with the religio-patriotic party in Israel and his dark moods rendered him peculiarly susceptible to fear and jealousy. David's acts and manner undoubtedly irritated him, although there is good ground in Jonathan's friendship and the subsequent conduct of David for rejecting the hypothesis that the latter was caught plotting. True, at a later period Saul is represented as bitterly complaining "that there is no one that discloseth to me when my son maketh a league with the son of Jesse" (I. Sam. xxii. 8); yet there is no warrant for regarding these words as more than an expression of the suspicions of a hyper-sensitive man, excited by the idle whispers which must have been current in the court during his later days.

97. Saul was too open-minded to succeed in removing the wily Judean by treachery. Meantime success followed David. By his marriage with Michal he became a prince of the royal family, second in rank to Jonathan. At last, when his servants refused to slay him, Saul himself, in one of his attacks of melancholia, flung a spear at the one against whom he had conceived such a strong suspicion and antipathy. David avoided the shaft; but it was clear that he must flee from the court, — the intercessions of his friend Jonathan could not save him. Naturally, he turned to his kinsmen for support. As he fled southward to Judah he stopped for refreshment with the priestly house of Eli, who had settled at Nob, just north of Jebus. He allayed the suspicions of the priests by declaring that

he was on the king's business, and that because of the
secrecy of the mission he had left his followers in concealment. Believing the prince, they did not hesitate
to give him of the shew-bread, which ordinarily was
reserved for the priests alone. Their courtesy cost
them their lives; for Doeg the Edomite, the royal
herdsman (the Iago of Hebrew history), was present
and witnessed their act. For some reason he had conceived such a bitter hatred toward the priests that
when Saul one day was holding court, and was especially irritated by the news of David's safe escape, this
Edomite recalled their deed of kindness to the outlaw. The king in a fit of anger summoned the
priests, and, without heeding their protestations of
innocence, commanded that they be slain. While the
Hebrews about him stood motionless, Doeg cut them
down. The whole family were thus slaughtered, with
the exception of Abiathar the son of Ahimelech, who
fled to David.

98. About the young outlaw gathered a heterogeneous band. The nucleus consisted of David's immediate kinsmen. Malcontents from Saul's court, debtors,
adventurers, and outlaws shared the fortunes of the
young champion; foreigners, as well as Hebrews, were
found fighting under his standard. At the fortress of
Adullam, which seems to have been located on the
western headlands of Judah, was his rallying point;
in the caves about he found the needed places of concealment. Only by conquest could he hope to retain
the loyalty of the freebooters who had espoused his
cause. The Canaanitish town of Keilah, situated on
the border-land between hill and plain, was besieged
by the Philistines: David proceeded to its relief,

thereby winning rich spoil and a temporary home.
But this border fortress was only a few hours from
Saul's capital, and the king's anger still pursued his
former armor-bearer. Therefore, in accordance with
the response of the oracle which he consulted, David
gave up his newly acquired stronghold just in time to
escape capture.

99. It is difficult to follow his subsequent wanderings. During the lulls in the Philistine warfare Saul
took occasion to follow David, in the hope that he
might entrap him. On one of these campaigns into
the Judean wilderness the pursuer fell into the hands
of the pursued; David, however, with the remarkable
moderation which characterized him, refused to use
violence to attain his ends, and consequently spared
the king's life. His forbearance was tested even more
by a certain Nabal, a descendant of the ancient Calebites, who lived at the town of Carmel, southeast of
Hebron, on the borders of the Judean desert. David's
followers had constituted themselves a kind of border-
guard, protecting Nabal's possessions from desert robbers. In accordance with the ways of the Orient, their
leader demanded a suitable reward for services rendered. Nabal, however, proving himself a churl, sent
back the messengers with a rude rebuff. His wife
alone saved him from dire retribution at the hands of
David's band by her prompt action in presenting the
desired gifts. Death soon removed Nabal, and paved
the way for a marriage between his wife Abigail and
David, — which brought to the outlaw chief not only
rich possessions in flocks, but also the support of the
strong tribe of Caleb.

100. Added possessions and followers increased

David's dangers on Hebrew soil. He began in time to tire of the life of an outlaw. In desperation, he threw himself upon the mercy of his hereditary foe, Achish, king of Gath. The friendly reception with which he was greeted is not altogether inexplicable. David, as the champion of the Hebrews, had inspired in the minds of the courageous Philistines a genuine respect. The enmity of Saul had driven him from the armies of Israel, yet the moment that Jonathan should succeed his father, the outlaw would again be at the head of the Hebrew host; they therefore hailed the defection of their old foe to their side as a great conquest. Ziklag, on the southwestern boundaries of Judah, was assigned to him as a residence. Although the Philistine king trusted him completely, David was attempting to play a difficult rôle. While professing entire loyalty to his new masters the Philistines, he was endeavoring to retain the affections of the Israelites. The records tell how, frequently going out ostensibly on a forage against the Hebrews, he fell upon his old foes the desert robbers, and, taking care to slay all the captives, returned, presenting the spoil as evidence of his hostility to his kinsmen. Even David, with all his cunning in deceiving, could not have kept up the illusion long. Fortunately for him it was not necessary.

9

IV

THE BATTLE OF GILBOA, AND THE DEATH OF SAUL

101. HAVING the champion of the Hebrews as their ally, the Philistine chiefs determined to strike a united blow against the weakened kingdom of Saul, and reestablish their superiority over the Hebrews. Accordingly, they rallied their forces and marched up along the coast, passed their old battle-field at Aphek, and took their position on the northern side of the plain of Esdraelon, near the town of Shunem. As the fief of Achish, king of Gath, David with his followers was summoned for the great rally against the Hebrews. He responded with apparent alacrity. What he would have done at the last moment is difficult to determine; it is exceedingly improbable that he would have raised his sword against his kinsmen. He was delivered from this dilemma, however, by the suspicions of the other Philistine chieftains, who did not have the unbounded trust in David that he had inspired in the king of Gath. Accordingly, Achish, after many apologies, invited the young Hebrew to withdraw. Although this deliverance was exactly what David was longing for, in complying he did not lose the opportunity to enter a protest.

His release proved most timely. On his return to Ziklag he found his city pillaged and laid in ruins by the Amalekites, — who had perhaps heard of the general call to arms, and had improved the occasion to be revenged upon their enemy. Rallying his followers, and encouraged by a favorable response from the oracle, David set out into the trackless desert in pursuit of the robbers. An Egyptian slave, whom the marauders had left behind to die, was found, and guided them to their foes. The Amalekites fell an unsuspecting prey to the sudden attack of David's warriors; and the Hebrews, recovering their families, returned with rich spoil. It is significant that a portion of David's share in the latter was sent in the form of gifts to the elders of Judah, and to the chiefs of the Jerachmeelites and Kenites, those southern tribes who had at this period almost completely assimilated with the Hebrews.

102. Meantime the hosts in the north were taking their position for the battle. The Hebrews were encamped just across the plain south of Shunem, at the foot of Gilboa. Here belongs the account of Saul's visit to the witch of Endor. It represents Israel's stalwart king on the eve before the battle as deserted by Jehovah. To his eager inquiries respecting the coming battle, answer came " neither by dreams, nor by Urim, nor by prophets." In his extremity he resolved to resort to one of the representatives of that ancient cult which he had endeavored to exterminate. In disguise and with only two attendants, he set out on his midnight journey. Making a detour to avoid the Philistine army, he finally reached the town of Endor, which nestles under the hill to the south of Mount Tabor, where a woman with a familiar spirit was found; and to her he applied. Notwithstanding his concealment, his height and broad shoulders naturally betrayed him. The woman first exacted a promise that he would not deliver her up to justice. Then he requested that

Samuel might be summoned. This she pretended to do. The scene and methods were quite similar to those of the modern heralds of departed spirits. It is nowhere stated that Saul himself saw Samuel. The message which the medium reported from the seer was what was clear in the light of the situation, — namely, defeat for the Hebrews. Saul, in whom there was a strong element of superstition, was overcome completely by the announcement. When he returned, it was to what he regarded as a hopeless fight against fate. His courage, however, stands out all the clearer with this dark background.

103. It is doubtful whether all the Hebrews rallied about their king in this last struggle. Certainly, there were many discontents in Israel. David's power and influence were growing, and none attached to him would be found at Gilboa. It is significant that the elders and chieftains of the south were apparently at home to receive David's gifts (sect. 101), and after the battle quickly hastened to make him their king. Against Saul were assembled all the Philistine forces, confident of victory. Israel's king having lost his enthusiasm could not, as of old, inspire his warriors. The battle seems to have been joined on the plain to the northeast of Gilboa. The details of the disastrous contest are not given. Before long the Hebrews were in flight, vainly seeking refuge upon the spurs of Mount Gilboa. Jonathan, and two other sons, fell by Saul's side. Almost deserted, afflicted by a shower of arrows and encircled by foes, the king commanded his armor-bearer to slay him, that he might not meet an ignominious fate at the hands of the Philistines. When his servant refused this last service, he fell upon his own sword. His

example was followed by his armor-bearer, and Israel's
enemies were left complete masters of the field. When
they searched the sides of Gilboa on the morrow, they
found the bodies of Saul and his sons, and hung them
in derision upon the walls of Bethshean near by. The
king's head and armor were borne away to their land
as trophies of victory. A deed of loving service is the
only ray which lights up the deep gloom which envel-
ops the last days of Israel's first king. In gratitude
for their former deliverance (sect. 90), the citizens of
Jabesh-gilead rescued the bodies from the walls of Bethshean and buried them with due honors within their
town.

104. The character and work of Saul has been vari-
ously estimated. In fact, as we have seen (sect. 77)
in our two great collections of old narratives in the
Book of I. Samuel, he is regarded with varying degrees
of favor. In chapters ix.–xiv. the sympathy of the
narrator is with Saul, while in the remainder of the
book the interest is with David; and consequently his
persecutor is viewed in no kindly light. These latter
records also explain in part the tendency which has
prevailed almost up to the present time to condemn
Saul completely. His relations with David were such
as to suggest a contrast. His own and later generations
idealized the character of Israel's conquering king; in
a corresponding manner that of Saul was depreciated.
Neither was wholly good, nor wholly bad; both shared
the weaknesses of their times, and both had their good
qualities as well as their faults. Saul was a simple-
minded, impulsive, courageous warrior; he was a loyal
patriot who loved his people and was ready to give his
life for them; his physical pre-eminence, combined with

energy and enthusiasm, fitted him to lead a sudden attack and to awaken loyal support, while his intrepid courage kindled the same in others. But Saul was a son of that rude age whose roots were found in the period of the judges. In a sense he was a child grown big. The position which he occupied demanded executive ability, tact, the power of organization, and, above all, patience and persistency. In these maturer qualities he was deficient; they are rarely the possession of fiery, impetuous natures. In addition, Saul was unable to understand and appreciate the higher religious experiences and ideals which were already becoming the possession of the more enlightened souls of seers like Samuel. As is frequently true with such a nature, Saul was superstitious. Circumstances tended to develop the darker rather than the brighter elements in his character. The constant trials and cares of the court and battle-field daunted his enthusiasm, and induced those attacks of melancholia which obscured the nobler Saul and led him to commit acts which constantly increased the density of the cloud that gathered about his latter days.

105. When he fell at Gilboa, and the Philistines again became masters of northern and central Canaan, Saul's work seemed to be completely undone; but its foundations were laid too deeply to be undermined by political changes. Saul found the Hebrews ground down under Philistine dominance, broken in spirit, undisciplined, and little more than cowards. He united and aroused them to strike for independence. By his successes he inspired in them confidence and courage. In the severe training-school of Philistine warfare, he developed out of the cowards who had fled before the

Philistine army to hide themselves in caves and cisterns the hardy, brave warriors with whom David made his conquests. Above all, he taught the Hebrews by practical illustration, more clearly than ever before, that by union and union alone they could be free, and enjoy peace and prosperity. As is often the case, the pioneer perished amidst seeming failure before he saw the ripe fruits of his labors; but his work was absolutely necessary. David reaped the fruits of Saul's sowing, but the harvest would never have been so glorious without the pioneer's toils.

DAVID KING OVER JUDAH, AND THE FALL OF THE
HOUSE OF SAUL

106. THE old records which have furnished so many
graphic pictures of David's experience during his outlaw period, have preserved few details respecting his
history during the next few years. When the news came
to him that Saul and his sons had fallen before their
foes on Gilboa, he refrained from any expression of joy,
although the fact brought to him recall from exile and
the opportunity for unlimited advancement. Prudence
dictated his action. He desired to stand before the people, not as the enemy, but as a member and the natural
heir of the house of Saul. Appreciating the bitterness
of the jealousy between the north and the south, he
clearly perceived that this was the only way in which
he, a Judean, could ever become the head of all the
tribes. Accordingly, he figured as the avenger of the
fallen king. The messenger who hastened to Ziklag to
announce the death of Saul was slain by David's own
hand, because his haste was in itself an imputation
that the champion of the Hebrews was hostile to their
dead leader (II. Kings iv. 10). The song of lamentation which David sang over "the mighty fallen"
tended to enlist the affection and loyalty of the Israelites. It certainly was politic, but no one can fully
appreciate its spirit and still doubt that it was also

prompted by a genuine feeling; his moderation in constantly refraining from attempting to seize the kingship by violence also gives force to his words.   The
ideas and language of the eulogy strongly support the
conclusion that it was preserved in Israel's collection
of national songs, " The Book of the Upright" (i. 18),
in substantially the same form in which it fell from
the lips of the warrior singer; its tone is that of a
loyal patriot who justly estimated Saul's services to
his people : —

> Thy glory, O Israel, is slain upon thy high places !
> How are the mighty fallen !
> Ye daughters of Israel, weep over Saul.
> Who clothed you in scarlet ?
> Who put ornaments of gold upon your apparel ? [1]

All feelings of personal wrong are forgotten : —

> Saul and Jonathan were lovely and pleasant in their lives,
> And in their death they were not divided.
> They were swifter than eagles,
> They were stronger than lions.
> How are the mighty fallen,
> And the weapons of war perished ! [2]

107. Although David honestly lamented the death
of his friend Jonathan, and willingly paid a high tribute to Saul, he did not hesitate a moment to enter into
their heritage.   Not only did the oracle of Jehovah,
which he consulted, command him to go up to the
cities of Judah, but circumstances also were favorable for his reception.   Already by his marriage with
Abigail he had allied himself with the southern tribes
and become a wealthy property-holder.   His kinsmen

---

[1] i. 19, 24.   [2] i. 23, 27.

naturally were eager to share the glory of his exalta-
tion. His gifts to the elders of Judah after the capture of the Amalekites (sect. 101) indicate that he had
spared no effort to win their favor. Now that Saul
was dead and the Philistines were masters of central
Canaan, the Judeans were only too glad to call their
tribesman and champion to be their king. Since he
was a vassal, in high favor with the Philistines, this
action insured to them peace, although not complete
independence. Accordingly, at the old capital and
chief city of the south, Hebron, David was formally
elected king of Judah.

108. It is evident that the new king from the first
aspired to the rule over all Israel. His ambition manifested itself, however, not by a war of conquest, but
by a diplomatic message of commendation to the citizens of Jabesh-gilead for their fidelity to the memory
of Saul (sect. 103). He also artfully suggested that
now that Saul their deliverer was dead, he would willingly become their king. But conditions in the north
were not yet ripe. Abner, Saul's general, succeeded
in rescuing from the ruins at Gilboa a few remnants
of the shattered kingdom. Central Canaan, however,
was in the hands of the Philistines. Judah and the
various southern clans that had accepted the rule of
David were lost to the house of Saul. Little remained
besides the east-Jordan tribes. Mahanaim, north of
the Jabbok, was made the political centre of the petty
kingdom. Ishbaal, the surviving son of Saul (who
was styled by later generations Ishbosheth), was placed
on the throne by his great-uncle, Abner. The king was
either a mere boy, or else pitiably inefficient. Abner,
consequently, was the real ruler.

109. To maintain the independence of this little state was a most difficult task. On the east were the hostile Ammonites; on the south were the Moabites, who never failed to take advantage of the weakness of their kinsmen the Hebrews; on the west the Philistines were strongly intrenched. It is possible that the continued existence of the east-Jordan kingdom is to be explained by the hypothesis that it paid tribute to the Philistines. David and the Judeans were regarded as rebels against Saul's house. If the latter had been strong enough, it doubtless would have subdued the southern kingdom; as it was, a constant feud was kept up between the two rival states. A record is preserved of only one of the many engagements which must have taken place. Near the pool of Gibeon a battle was fought, in which the northern forces were put to flight. In the pursuit the youngest brother of Joab, Asahel, — who was "light of foot as one of the roes that are in the field," — seeking to win glory, pressed Abner so closely that the old warrior was forced to slay him in self-defence. Even though he was justified in his act, he had spilt blood; and, according to the unreasonable laws of blood-revenge, his blood must be shed in requital. From the first the civil war seems to have been little more than a feud between Abner and Joab. David held himself aloof from these contests; in fact, as subsequent events proved, they threatened to be suicidal to his hope of finally becoming king over all the tribes. Circumstances, however, were gradually paving the way for the realization of his ambitions. His policy of waiting was vindicated. The continued existence of the east-Jordan state could be secured only by a constant and

well-nigh hopeless struggle against the strong enemies that surrounded it.   Meantime, its resources were being exhausted.

110. On the other hand, during these seven years of war David's influence and prestige were growing. Many in Northern Israel began to realize that he was the only one who could secure for them deliverance, and to long to see him king over united Israel. This party found an unexpected leader in Abner himself. He had been faithful to the house of Saul; but Ishbaal, in a fit of envy, accused him of treachery in plotting for the throne.   Ordinarily, marriage with the wife of a dead king was regarded as equivalent to entering a claim to the power of the deceased; Abner's relations with Rizpah (Saul's concubine), however, were not sufficient evidence to justify the charge. The result was that Abner, who may have been only awaiting a pretext, entered at once into negotiations with David in behalf of the elders of Northern Israel.   The Judean king, appreciating that he was master of the situation, stipulated that his former wife, Michal (Saul's daughter), should be restored to him before he listened to any definite proposals. His purpose is manifest: as the acknowledged son-in-law of Saul, he would again stand before the Israelites as the rightful heir of their former king. Ishbaal, helpless in the hand of Abner, accorded with his demand, and Michal was torn from her sorrowing family.

111. The union of the tribes seemed about to be amicably consummated. Abner went to Hebron to complete the plans. David, fearing trouble, had apparently sent Joab away on a foray, but he returned just after Abner had departed. Learning of his visit,

David's relentless general entered a complaint with
the king because he had trusted Abner. When this
made no impression, he sent a messenger to recall his
rival. With superlative treachery, Joab received him
in a friendly manner at the gate of Hebron, and then
taking him aside foully murdered him on the pretext
of blood-revenge. At this early period it is evident
that David was not the real master in Israel. Instead
of punishing the murderer, he only called down curses
upon his head for his deed of perfidy.

112. By this act all hope of a united Israel seemed
lost. The representative of the northern tribes had
been basely slain in David's capital. But the king
was innocent, and he made no delay in proclaiming it.
In sackcloth he loudly lamented over the grave of
Abner, refusing all food until nightfall; his action and
song of lamentation were accepted by the northern
tribes as a peace-offering and an earnest of fidelity.
Another crime at this crisis furthered the cause of
David. Two Benjaminite captains, thinking to win
favor, fell upon Ishbaal, and beheading him brought
this gory proof of their treachery to Hebron. They
entirely mistook the character and mood of David.
From the first he had posed, not as the enemy,
but as the champion of the house of Saul. He therefore hastened to pour out the blood of the murder-
ers as a further peace-offering; their hands and feet
were hung beside the pool of Hebron as an expression of David's abhorrence of the deed, and the head
of Ishbaal was interred in the grave of Abner. Deprived of their king and general, and encircled by
strong enemies, there remained for the northern and
eastern tribes but one means of deliverance. Of this

they hastened to avail themselves. The seven and one-half years of civil discord and struggle had again demonstrated that division meant national distress, and that without a king who could command and organize, foreign bondage was unavoidable. This, therefore, represented real progress; for the proud spirit of the house of Joseph being broken, and the ancient jealousy between the tribes for the time being smothered, Israel was on the eve of her most glorious epoch.

VI

DAVID ESTABLISHED AS KING OVER ALL ISRAEL

113. AT Hebron David was again anointed king.
This time a solemn covenant was formed, binding together all the Israelitish tribes in allegiance to the son
of Jesse. In accepting the fealty of the elders of the
northern clans, David practically renounced his vas-
salage to the Philistines; for before he could become
in reality king over his new heritage, this foreign yoke
must be shaken off. Like Saul, his predecessor, he
could rule indisputably only after he had won his
kingdom by the sword. The Philistines, recognizing
the significance of his election, immediately poured
their forces into central and southern Israel. The
records are strangely silent respecting the details of
this war of independence. The account of the deeds
of David's heroes in II. Samuel xxiii. 8–39 supplies
certain interesting data. From these it is evident that
David was caught unprepared. The Philistines over-
ran Judah and even captured Bethlehem, forcing
David, as during his outlaw days, to take refuge in
the cave of Adullam. But the Hebrew king was
familiar with the land and with his foes. In the guerilla warfare to which he was obliged to resort, the advantage was with the Israelites. Gradually they
gained in strength, as they rallied in ever-increasing
numbers about their king. The Philistines, unable to

maintain themselves permanently among the barren Judean hills, were forced to retire. Repeatedly they marched up through the valley of Rephaim, which leads to the north of Jebus, and were met and defeated by the Hebrews. At last, near Gibeon, the Philistines were completely routed, and driven from the territory of Israel, even to Gezer on the plain. The victory was so overwhelming that the Israelites were effectually and forever delivered from the invasions of this foe, which for more than a generation had sapped their national life and threatened them with utter annihilation.

114. The biblical narrative gives few hints respecting the order of events in David's reign. The next step probably was the capture of the stronghold of Jebus. Even down to the days of David, certain Canaanitish tribes had remained in undisturbed possession of their towns and lands. As the Hebrews grew in strength, they began to look with envious eyes upon the possessions of these earlier masters of the land. According to II. Samuel xxi. Saul, disregarding the ancient treaty, attacked the Canaanitish town of Gibeon; later, Solomon reduced the Canaanites to serfdom. David, in seeking a site for his new capital, recognized the peculiar advantages of Jebus, which was located on the northern boundaries of Judah, and held by a local Canaanitish tribe. Like other important towns of that age it had a citadel, to which the people fled when attacked. This was regarded as impregnable. Its strength was due to its situation. It was probably located at Ophel, the spur of rock which extends southward from the hill, which was defended on the east by the Kidron valley, and on the west by

the Tyropœan. These two valleys met toward the south, so that the only vulnerable point was toward the north, where a high wall would naturally be built. A perennial spring (now known as the Virgin's Fount) determined the location of the town and furnished water, which is so rare among the hills of Judah.

115. David, as king of Israel, demanded peaceable possession of the Jebusite stronghold. Trusting in the strength of their position, the inhabitants tauntingly suggested that the blind and lame of their town alone would be able to protect it from attack. Accepting the implied challenge, David urged his men to the assault, and speedily captured it. Some of the natives, at least, he left in possession of their land, for at a subsequent period he purchased the Temple site from Araunah the Jebusite (II. Sam. xxiv. 16–25). The stronghold, however, he took, and, fortifying it, made it his capital; among his contemporaries it was known as "the city of David." The importance of this act cannot be overestimated; it is one of the best illustrations of David's foresight and executive ability. If he had retained the Judean town of Hebron as his capital, it is doubtful whether he would ever have been able to command the loyal allegiance of the jealous house of Joseph. Not only was Jebus more centrally located, but it was captured and rechristened as the common possession of all the tribes. Its location, on the border between Judah and Benjamin, was suggestive of the union between the north and the south, of which it was the seal. Past it ran the highways of inland trade. Its natural strength made it a fitting centre for the political life of the Hebrew kingdom, which was crystallizing about it.

116. David, following the example of former rulers, proceeded to make his city also the religious centre of his state. To this end he assembled his army, and with great pomp escorted the Ark from the place where it had been left after its return from the Philistines. The undertaking, however, was for a time abandoned because of the sudden death of Uzziah, one of the attendants, as he reached out his hand to keep the sacred symbol from falling. The Hebrews regarded this as a token of Jehovah's displeasure; but when marked prosperity came to Obed-edom the Gittite, at whose house it was left, they again took courage to bring it into the city of David. While the procession advanced, the king sacrificed an ox and a fatling every six paces, and girded with a linen ephod, he "danced before the Lord with all his might." Amidst shouting and the blare of trumpets, the Ark was brought to the tent prepared for it within the city. Its arrival was celebrated by a great national festival, at which the king himself sacrificed burnt-offerings and peace-offerings, and distributed plentifully to the people. This simple act is one of the most important events in human history; for in establishing a royal shrine at his new capital, David made Jerusalem the city of religions, the supreme religious sanctuary of half humanity.

VII

DAVID'S FOREIGN WARS AND CONQUESTS

117. AFTER David had freed his land from the foreign invader and consolidated his kingdom, he turned his attention to foreign conquest. In the midst of the hostile foes which encircled the Hebrews, conquest was the only guaranty of immunity from attack. At this time a lull in the invasions from Egypt and Assyria, due to the weakness of these world-powers, gave David an opportunity to become master of the Canaanitish world without foreign opposition. During his long and varied experience, first as an outlaw and then as king of Judah, he had gathered about him a brave and tried band of warriors. Chief among them was his commander, Joab. This warrior was a man of blood, who never hesitated to take the life of one who stood in his way. If he had no fear of moral laws, he certainly knew no fear of man. Combined with an intrepid courage, he possessed rare skill as a military commander. His faults were many, and he often acted counter to David's orders, yet from first to last he was loyal to the best interests of his king; to him David largely owed his military successes and the conquests which made his reign glorious. Next in honor stood the thirty-seven heroes who had each distinguished themselves by acts of daring during the Philistine wars. Also attached to the person of the monarch, and constituting his body-guard, was the band of six hundred hired mercenaries, called the Pelethites, Cherethites, and Gittites; their name indicates that they were for the most part Philistines. It is at first surprising to note that Israel's beloved king trusted his personal safety, not to his countrymen, but to foreigners, — who, like the Papal Swiss guard of to-day, knew no master but the one who paid them; but even during the lifetime of David its necessity was demonstrated. Over this body-guard was placed Benaiah, who by virtue of his position stood next to Joab, the commander-in-chief. In time of war, when the militia was called out, the thirty-seven heroes who had distinguished themselves in former campaigns were probably placed in command of the different companies. The presence of the experienced six hundred also gave confidence to the entire host. With such an army it was not strange that David rapidly extended his boundaries.

118. Another advantage resulting from conditions in the Canaanitish world was that David was able to deal with his adversaries, not all at once, but in turn. The land of Moab was overrun, and its inhabitants were treated with that barbarity which was characteristic of the age. The fate of the Edomites was even worse. Near the Dead Sea a great battle was fought, in which they were defeated, and according to I. Kings xi. 15, 16 all the males were put to death. Hebrew garrisons were established throughout the territory of the conquered peoples to hold them in subjection. The wandering desert robbers, the Amalekites, were pursued by David with a relentlessness which was doubtless intensified because of his previous encounters with them; they were so thoroughly exterminated that they

THE
HEBREW EMPIRE
UNDER DAVID

Sidon

Tyre

PHOENICIANS

Litani R.

Hamath R.

ZOBAH

Hermon Mt.

Damascus

Abel

Dan

ARGOB

Hazor

Sea of
Chinnereth

Shunem

Megiddo

Yarmuk R.

Beth-shean

Mahanaim (?)

Jabesh Gilead

GREAT   SEA

River Kishon

Mt. Carmel

Shechem

Jabbok R.

AMMONITES

Joppa

Baalath

Gibeon

Bethel

Jericho

Goba

Jerusalem

Gilgal

Rabbath Ammon

Ekron

Gezer

Ajalon

Beth-horon

Gath

Askelon

Heshbon

Adullam

SALT SEA

Keilah

Gaza

PHILISTINES

Hebron

Engedi

Arnon R.

MOABITES

Beersheba

Ziklag

Tamar (?)

Kir Moab

River of Egypt

EDOMITES

Bozrah

ARABIAN   DESERT

Sela

Ezion-geber
RED SEA   Elath

Longitude East   36   from Greenwich

never figure again in Hebrew history. Thus the sword of David was potent, even to the Red Sea.

119. His aggressive foreign policy was already generally recognized. Otherwise his ambassadors, sent with a message of condolence, would not have been treated so shamefully by the Ammonite king. Suspecting some hostile purpose, the latter practically declared war against David, by sending back his messengers, each stripped and shorn on one side. This gauntlet was quickly taken up, and Joab, at the head of an army, was despatched against them. Meantime they had hired their neighbors, the men of Tob and Maacah and the Arameans from the north (known as Syrians in the English version), to come to their aid. On their arrival the Israelites found themselves exposed to a double attack, with the Ammonites on their front and the Arameans in their rear. At this crisis Joab's generalship saved the day. Dividing his forces into two divisions, with back to back so as mutually to support each other, he led one line against the Arameans, while the other, under his brother, faced the Ammonites. Joab, as usual, was successful; and the Ammonites, perceiving the flight of their allies, retired within their city. Their strongly fortified towns enabled them to hold out several years against the Israelitish armies which were sent against them. In the second campaign the Ammonites summoned other Arameans, but in vain; for they were put to flight, and those to whose assistance they had come were left a prey to David's warriors. At last their capital, Rabbath-Ammon, surrendered. The Arameans who had been called in to aid the Ammonites were forced to acknowledge David's rule. It is difficult to deter-

mine from the records just how far this extended. The
Arameans beyond Mount Hermon and about Damascus
seem to have retained their independence by paying
tribute to David during his lifetime.

120. Between the peoples on the north and east and
the Hebrews the relations were most friendly. Toi, king
of Hamath between the Lebanons, rejoicing that David
had humbled his enemies the Arameans of Zobah, sent
him messages of congratulation. Hiram, king of Tyre,
appreciating the advantages that would accrue from an
alliance with the rising Hebrew state, readily furnished
materials and workmen to build a palace for David.
After their first bitter struggles were over, the Israelites and Philistines lived amicably side by side;
many of David's most trusted warriors and friends
were Philistines. Thus at last the Israelites were
freed from all fear of hostile attack, for they were
masters of the Canaanitish world. From Philistia
and Phœnicia to the Arabian desert on the east, and
from the Lebanons to the Red Sea, David's sway was
absolute. The political power of the Hebrews had
reached its zenith.

VIII

THE ORGANIZATION OF DAVID'S KINGDOM

121. THE empire which David succeeded in founding was, like the kingdom of Saul, military in its genesis and organization. David had been called by the Israelites to be their civil head because he had proved himself able to lead their armies to victory. In the simplicity of the earlier days his functions were also for the most part military; his capital was at first little more than a fortress, and the chief obligation which his subjects in turn acknowledged to their king was to respond to the call to arms when a war threatened. But David's foreign acquisitions made a more complicated organization necessary. Side by side with the conquests of his foes by the sword came the peaceful conquest of those Israelites living on the outskirts of Canaan, who in their long and difficult struggle for the possession of the soil, had almost forgotten the rest of their kinsmen. For the first time in their history they recognized the bond of common blood and religion, and became in reality a part of the Hebrew state; their accession swelled the ranks of the Israelites, and perhaps partially explains David's desire to take a census of his people. Joab, the captain of the host, was detailed to attend to it. Although he seems to have included many of the dependent peoples, his report — eight hundred thousand fighting men in Israel and five hundred thousand in Judah — is almost in-

credible. The round numbers, at least, suggest that it
was only a general estimate, such as the time devoted
to the census — nine months and twenty days — alone
made possible.

122. As has been frequently illustrated in Hebrew
history, the Israelites of this age, in common with their
contemporaries, always interpreted a public misfortune
as an indication that the deity had been displeased; and
it was the duty of their priests and seers to explain in
what respect the people had erred. When a drought
for three years afflicted Israel, it was announced, apparently by the priestly oracle (II. Sam. xxi. 1), that
it was because Saul's wrong to the Gibeonites had been
left unavenged. Ignorant of the truth that Jehovah
takes no pleasure in human sacrifice, they hung the
seven sons of Saul out under the heavens, until the
rain at last came, which they regarded as an index that
Jehovah's wrath had been appeased. Similarly, when
a pestilence afflicted the land of Israel it was associated with the census which had been recently taken at
David's command. The ancient narrative in II. Sam.
xxiv. even declares that Jehovah moved David to
number the people because "his anger was kindled
against Israel." The author of this passage, however,
gives no hint as to why the anger of the Lord was
kindled against Israel, nor what was the nature of
David's sin. Being ignorant of the teaching of the
Book of Job and of later prophets, he, with his contemporaries, regarded a calamity as a certain indication
that a sin had been committed. Perhaps he also shared
the Oriental superstition against numbering, or, more
probably, associated this census of David with the subsequent unpopular division of the people for purposes
of taxation.

123. The favorable issue of David's wars brought not only added numbers, but also increased wealth for Israel. Peace and prosperity went hand in hand. Rich tribute also flowed into the public treasury. The close diplomatic relations with the surrounding peoples made it necessary to constitute new offices. The Royal Scribe — who corresponded to the modern Secretary of State, or Chancellor — was Seraiah. Events in the national life had begun to assume such importance that the office of State Recorder, or Chronicler, was created; during David's reign this was held by Jehoshaphat, the son of Ahilud. Among the nobles and state counsellors was found the prophet Nathan. The royal priests — Ahimelech the son of Abiathar, and Zadok the son of Ahitub — were also court officials. David's sons are likewise referred to as priests (II. Sam. viii. 18).

124. Among the ever-increasing throng which constituted the court was Jonathan's son, Meribaal, who is known in II. Samuel by the later name of Mephibosheth. When a child he had met with an accident, as his nurse fled with him after the fall of his father at Gilboa, and ever since that time, as the result, had been lame. His boyhood had been spent in retirement at Lo-debar, east of the Jordan. He, alone of the house of Saul, had escaped the bloody sacrifice at Gibeon. David, seeking to do honor to the memory of his friend Jonathan, in time sought out Meribaal and restored to him his ancestral possessions. His infirmity incapacitated him for the kingship. David, however, took the precaution of bringing him to his court, where he had a place at the king's table. In this simple manner the military camp of the Judean prince grew into an Oriental court, and the Hebrew peasants were organized into a powerful empire.

IX

DAVID'S FAMILY HISTORY

125. THE domestic history of David presents a sad contrast to the political. The harem, with its attendant evils, is in part responsible for this. By an aspiring prince like David, marriage was regarded as one of the most efficient means of gaining influence and wealth. The temptation to multiply wives was strong. While king at Hebron, David had at least six wives, and subsequently added still others to his harem. The mother of his first-born, Amnon, was Ahinoam the Jezreelitess. His second, Chileab, the son of Abigail, must have died in his youth, for he does not appear in the later history. His third son, born at Hebron, was Absalom, the child of a foreign princess, — Maacah, the daughter of Talmai, king of Geshur. The fourth was Adonijah, the son of Haggith, probably an Israelitess. Altogether the names of seventeen sons, born to David by his different wives, are mentioned.

126. During the earlier part of his reign as king over all Israel, while the Ammonite war was in progress, David committed the double sin of deliberate adultery and murder, which blackened his hitherto fair record. It is true that, according to the ideas of the Orient, the monarch was privileged to take as his wife any of the daughters of the land; but already the Hebrews knew a higher standard, and the rudeness of

his age does not palliate the sin of adultery even in a
king. Although Bathsheba readily abetted him in his
intrigue, David consciously transgressed ; this is demonstrated by the efforts which he made to cover his
crime, — efforts which resulted in the murder of Uriah,
the one whom he had most deeply wronged. But the
king, instead of repenting for his heinous act, proceeded
to take Bathsheba into his harem. The knowledge of
his crime soon became public. Then it was, according
to the record, that Nathan the prophet and royal counsellor, as the messenger of the God of righteousness,
came before the king with the parable of the poor man
who was deprived of his one lamb by the rich and
powerful robber. While David was denouncing the
deed of injustice, condemnation fell on his own guilty
head. To refute the charge was impossible : the royal
culprit admitted that he had sinned. There is little,
however, in these words and in his subsequent life to
indicate that his repentance was as deep as it is sometimes pictured, although in the light of his age and
position it is remarkable. He passionately besought
Jehovah that the child of his sin might be spared.
Bathsheba's baneful influence continued to rule the
king, until in his old age she induced him to set
aside his eldest son and to nominate her child as his
successor.

127. David's sins, and the weakness of which they
were the expression, certainly darkened the latter years
of his reign. Israel's champion and idol, the one who
was regarded as the personification of all that was best
and noblest, had broken the holiest laws known to man.
If he, the most favored, thus fell, what could be expected of the ignorant masses? The degeneracy of

Solomon's reign is also largely traceable to this example of the "mighty fallen," but not gloriously. In David's immediate family history the evil results of his weakness are even more obvious. Impelled by lust, the eldest son, Amnon, basely deceived and wronged his half-sister, Tamar. Instead of, at least, compelling him to make reparation to her for the wrong in the manner dictated by the usages of the times, David, ignoring the duties of king and father, merely rebuked him. His criminal leniency cost the life of his first-born. Absalom, the own brother of Tamar, perhaps only too ready to find a pretext to remove his older brother, who stood in the way of his succession, espoused her cause. Two years he waited, until suspicions were allayed; then he invited his brothers to a great feast at his estate at Baal-Hazor in Ephraim. When Amnon was half drunk with wine, Absalom gave the signal to his servants, and they slew him.

128. Slowly but relentlessly this stupendous tragedy unfolds. Absalom fled to his mother's father, the king of Geshur, and remained there three years. David, in time forgetting the murder of Amnon, began to long for his exiled son. Joab, perceiving this, secured his recall through the cunning offices of a certain wise woman of Tekoa. She, employing the methods of Nathan (sect. 126), appealed to the king's compassion and induced him to commit himself to a certain principle, which she in turn demanded that he apply to the case of his son. Absalom, as a consequence, was allowed to return, and in time was received back into royal favor. The spoiled favorite soon conceived the idea of seizing the supreme power for himself. To that end he secured a chariot and body-guard of fifty

runners, with which to impress the people whenever
he appeared in public. His princely figure and bearing were also in his favor. During his latter days the
old king, neglecting his functions as supreme judge of
the empire, shrank more and more from the public gaze.
This opportunity the aspiring prince improved, whis-
pering in the ears of those who came up to the king
for judgment that their case was good, and hinting
that they would receive their dues if only he were
their judge. For four years Absalom systematically
courted popularity, and succeeded in winning it,
although his rival was Israel's conqueror king.

129. At the old Judean capital, Hebron, the conspiracy was launched. Thither Absalom invited all
his sympathizers and many others, who were thus un-
suspectingly involved. Almost all the nobles of the
court were with Absalom when he was proclaimed
king. It is a surprising fact that David's kinsmen,
the Judeans, were at first the chief supporters of the
rebel; many from the other tribes also quickly rallied
about his standard. The plot had been so carefully
developed that David was taken entirely unprepared.
In haste he set out from Jerusalem, accompanied by
his wives and the faithful body-guard, who saved him
at this crisis. Joab and a certain Ittai, a Gittite, also
remained true to the king. The priests Abiathar and
Zadok accompanied him, bearing the Ark. David,
however, bade them return with it to the city, trusting
his cause to Jehovah, even though the visible symbol
of his presence was in the hands of the conspirators.
His old energy and diplomatic skill returned in the
crisis; he sent back his trusted counsellor, Hushai,
with commands to profess allegiance to Absalom, and

by flattery and false advice to defeat the plans of the
rebel. The secret hatred of the house of Saul was
manifested at this time. Ziba, the servant of Meribaal, came to David with the news that his master had
decided to cast his lot with the conspirator. Even
more marked was the enmity of a certain Benjaminite
by the name of Shemei, who pursued him with bitter
curses and reproaches for his treatment of the sons of
Saul.

130. Meantime Absalom, with a huge following,
entered unopposed into the possession of Jerusalem.
Ahithophel, a Judean and the most respected counsellor
of the realm, urged him to pursue at once and smite
the defenceless king; but David was delivered at this
critical moment by the cunning of Hushai. Appealing
to the fear and vanity of Absalom, he suggested that it
would be unwise to attack the desperate men about
David, and that a far safer plan would be, assembling
all the Israelites, to crush him without danger or
trouble. Ahithophel, perceiving that in following this
counsel Absalom was rejecting his supreme opportunity, in chagrin committed suicide. By the sons of
the priests, Hushai informed David concerning the
progress of events in this city, and warned him to
hasten his flight.

131. It is interesting to note that the east-Jordan
tribes, who had been last to forsake the house of Saul,
remained truest to the exiled king. At Mahanaim he
took his stand. The chieftains of Gilead rallied about
him with their forces; the subject king of the Ammonites also came to his assistance. Among the fugitives who had accompanied him from Jerusalem were
found the military leaders of Israel, so that his army

was quickly organized. In the forest of Ephraim, east
of the Jordan, the decisive battle was fought. David's
followers in their devotion would not permit him to
take part in the engagement. His army was divided
into three divisions, — under Joab, Abishai his brother,
and Ittai the Gittite. Absalom's commander was
Amasa, the son of an Ishmaelite. David's forces
were victorious. In the flight, Absalom was caught
by his hair in the branches of a terebinth. When this
was reported to Joab he hastened to slay him, totally
disregarding the strict injunctions of his king. By this
act the battle was ended.

132. The rejoicing over the victory was saddened
by the bitter lamentations of the bereaved father.
Discontent began to spread among the people. Joab,
not without reason, rebuked the king for his action,
and warned him against the consequences. Awaken-
ing to his duty, David endeavored to conciliate his
subjects ; but the old rivalry and jealousy between
the houses of Judah and Joseph had again broken out.
The northern tribes took the initiative in bringing back
their king, while the Judeans held aloof in sullen
silence. To reconcile them and free himself from the
power of Joab, which had become so odious to him,
David invited his own tribe to escort him back to his
capital, and appointed Amasa, the captain of the defeated army, as his commander-in-chief. A general
amnesty was granted to all the rebels ; even Shemei
was not excepted. Suspecting Meribaal's protestations
that he had been wrongfully misrepresented by his servant, the king restored to him only half his possessions, and refrained from further inquiry. Those who
had been true to him in his time of danger were richly
rewarded,

133. Although there was great rejoicing over the restoration of their hero, the jealousy between the north and the south repeatedly flamed up, and finally the favors shown to the tribe of Judah kindled it into a blaze. The leader of this rebellion was Sheba, a Benjaminite. The spirit of revolt spread throughout the north. David commanded Amasa to rally his forces and suppress it, but the Hebrews were reluctant to follow the leader of an unsuccessful rebellion. Joab, whose hands had been stained by many a murder, treacherously slew his rival, and gathering the forces of David hunted the rebels to the city of Abel, in the north, where their leader was killed and the insurrection quelled. Joab's energy and military ability preserved the unity of Israel, and again secured for himself the position which he had held so long. The few remaining years of David's reign passed peacefully. The old king retired more and more from public life as his powers relaxed, until he finally handed over his authority to his son Solomon.

X

134. In the David of history the elements of strength and weakness peculiar to his age find their clearest illustration. His versatility and tendency to do everything in the superlative explain why different generations and individuals have regarded him with such varying degrees of favor. As a matter of fact, his character was neither that of the Christian saint nor of the designing villain. The two opposite tendencies — either to condone his faults while idealizing his virtues, or to try and condemn him before the bar of modern ethics — are equally unjust and misleading. He was a man of his times, and should therefore be measured by the standards of his own day. In so doing, the mistake of holding up an imperfect character as a model for the present is avoided, and at the same time a true estimate of the real David is gained. It must be remembered constantly that he was removed from the period of the judges by only one generation. The years of bitter warfare which joined the days of Gideon and David were not calculated to soften the barbarity of Israel's pioneer epoch. When an enlightened seer like Samuel hewed a captured enemy into pieces (I. Sam. xv.), little clemency can be expected from a conquering king. We shudder when we read of David's treatment of the subjugated Moabites and

Edomites, and yet he was only acting in accordance with the practices of the old Semitic world. He did not hesitate on many occasions to pervert the truth when an object was to be gained; in the words of Saul, "he was able to deal very subtly." To the priests of Nob and his Philistine patron, Achish king of Gath, he deliberately made misrepresentations; but he lived among a people who at that stage in their development regarded the ability to deceive successfully as almost a virtue. Even to-day the proverb, "A lie is the salt of a man," voices the sentiment of the Orient. The means which David used to secure the kingship of all Israel certainly are laudable compared with those which were then in vogue. The defects, which we who stand in the full light of New Testament revelation so deeply deplore, commended rather than condemned David in the eyes of his contemporaries. Of all his recorded acts, two alone fall far below the standards which were known at that time. The dethroned tyrants, Lust and Murder, who had ruled supreme over primitive man, for the time being mastered Israel's king. As we have seen, they gained the ascendency under the guise of those current Oriental ideas according to which a monarch was regarded as the irresponsible master of his subjects. But David as a Hebrew king was responsible both to his people and to Jehovah, the God of righteousness; against both he sinned consciously. It is sad to note the effects upon the royal culprit of these crimes and the circumstances which led up to them. In his later days David is not nearly so attractive as the shepherd boy who by gradual steps came to the throne of Israel.

135. While David's crimes against society were the most culpable, the greatness and breadth of his character were demonstrated by his repentance. The narrative does not suggest that he felt any such overpowering sense of sin as came to the enlightened Hebrews of a later age; but the sight of a conquering monarch humbly confessing his sins was unprecedented. It bespoke a high degree of moral sensibility, and furnished most unequivocal evidence that he recognized the law of Jehovah as superior to that of his own royal will. The recognition of this divine law is the key to the understanding of his character. He was naturally gifted with a rare grace and winsomeness; but these qualities alone do not call forth such loyalty as he evoked from his associates and followers. The friendship of Jonathan is a lofty tribute to David's nobility. He had but to express a wish for a drink of water from the well at Bethlehem, and three of his heroes, at the cost of their lives, fought their way through the ranks of the Philistines to secure it (II. Sam. xxiii. 15–18). Absalom's rebellion demonstrated that there were many in his court, foreigners as well as Israelites, who were attached to him simply by the bonds of personal affection. The fidelity of those with whom he came into closest contact was a far higher testimonial to David's genuineness than the eulogies of subsequent generations. His magnanimity is illustrated by his action in sparing the life of his persecutor, Saul, and by his graciously forgiving the rebel Shemei, who had made himself exceedingly obnoxious (II. Sam. xix. 18–23). It is not improbable that the command to Solomon to slay Shemei and Joab were put into the mouth of the

dying king by a later editor, who sought thereby to justify Solomon's subsequent acts; if it originally proceeded from David's lips, it was due to the childish spite of a dotard. In courage also, of which magnanimity is the complement, David was not lacking. This was demonstrated not only during his youth, when he won the title of champion of the Israelites, but also in his old age, when he was eager to lead his forces against the rebellion headed by Absalom (II. Sam. xviii. 2). The quality, however, which was rarest in his day, and which was one of the chief elements of his strength, was moderation. It found expression in a careful regard for human life, at least for that of the Israelites; the water secured from the well of Bethlehem at the risk of the lives of his followers he poured on the ground. Unlike most aspirants for power, he was content to wait. Although his followers advocated violence, Saul was safe in his hands, and Ishbaal was allowed to rule undisturbed by him until the elders of the northern tribes themselves called him to the throne of all Israel. His moderation was begotten by a keen sense of justice, which fitted him to decide with equity the cases that were brought to him as the supreme judge of the realm. Thus in the person of the son of Jesse were found those elements of courage, generosity, moderation, and justice which made him the great national hero of the Hebrews. Although his character was not above reproach, it was far above the average standards of his age, and was an earnest of that perfection which found its only and complete realization in the Son of Man.

136. In his religious life, the David of history ap-

pears to have been subject also to the limitations of his day. It is dangerous to derive a conception of his heart-life from the Psalms whose connection with Israel's illustrious king depends solely upon the doubtful testimony of their superscriptions. That he was a poet is attested by his lamentation over Saul and Jonathan, and later over Abner. His skill as a musician was well established. In antiquity the player commonly sang a song, frequently improvised, to the accompaniment of his instrument. Amos speaks of those who " devise for themselves instruments of music like David," indicating that in the centuries following the division of the kingdom David was regarded as the inventor of musical instruments, or at least as a patron of music. A lover of song and a poet, it would be strange indeed if he had not given expression to his religious sentiments in verse. Therefore it is probable in the light of history that some of the psalms in the Psalter came from him; just how many, is one of the most baffling problems in Old Testament study. It is evident that the question of the authorship of each psalm must be decided independently, by a comparison of the thought with the David of history and the degree of religious enlightenment of which he gives evidence. When a psalm abounds in the form of expression and deep spiritual ideas which represent the rich fruitage of the teaching of such prophets as Amos, Hosea, and Isaiah, the superscription " A Psalm of David" must be interpreted like the term " The Law of Moses " (sect. 30), " The Proverbs of Solomon " in the Book of Proverbs (sect. 152), or the title of the apocryphal book " The Wisdom of Solomon," as a general designation for a type of literature which was closely associated with the name of its earliest and most illustrious contributor and patron.

137. In studying the religious life of King David, it is essential not to be misled by the words which later prophetic historians, guided more by the religious than by the historical sense, have put into the mouth of their hero. No one certainly would be so hasty as to criticise their action in this respect, for it renders their narratives graphic, making them more real and truer pictures of the actual conditions than a dull chronicle of events; at the same time, by these means their didactic purpose is conserved far better. His recorded deeds, however, more than the words attributed to him, introduce us to the inner sanctuary of David's soul. If he had stood in the full light of prophetic teaching, it is doubtful whether he would have committed his dark crimes; surely, the spiritual light within him was not strong enough to reveal the heinousness of deceit and of cruelty to his enemies. At the same time, it is clear that he was one who deeply and genuinely feared Jehovah; in this respect he was far in advance of the kings who preceded and immediately followed him. His religious instincts, however, found expression in external forms rather than in those soul-throbs which are reflected in certain of the most spiritual psalms of the Psalter. For example, whenever he entered upon an important undertaking, instead of going directly to Jehovah in prayer, he consulted him through the priestly oracle. He hastened to bring the Ark of Jehovah to his new capital, that the symbol of the God whom he served might be with him. While this was being carried within the city of David, the old

record tells us that "he danced before the Lord with all his might." As we see him dancing and leaping before the Lord, we recognize that his piety is genuine; at the same time, we have no reason to believe that his faith was radically different from that of his contemporaries. In fact, when we find that he yielded apparently without a protest to the superstition of his age, and allowed the innocent sons of Saul to be "hung up unto the Lord in Gibeah" (II. Sam. xxi. 6), we feel, not that he was a treacherous hypocrite, but that he had not yet gained that intimate acquaintance with the Jehovah who revealed himself to later generations as the one who had no delight in sacrifice nor in burnt-offering, and whose tender mercies were so unlimited that he would blot out the greatest transgression (Psalms li. 16, 17). According to his light, David served the Jehovah whom he knew with marvellous fidelity and constancy. The idea of a theocracy was first formulated by later ages, yet during his reign it was first practically realized. He ruled over the united Hebrew tribes as Jehovah's representative. In his name he fought the battles against Israel's foes, whom he regarded as Jehovah's also. Contrary to the traditions of his day he established a new sanctuary at his capital. From the spoils which he won in his wars he provided the means wherewith to build a fitting dwelling-place for the God of his nation. The priests found in him a generous patron, and prophets like Nathan were among his most trusted counsellors. To do the will of Jehovah, as it was revealed to him, was the dominating principle of his life. More cannot be said of any one.

138. Combined with David's personal charms and genuine piety was a rare executive ability. He not

only understood but was also able to command men. His varied experiences as shepherd, courtier, outlaw, and vassal-prince had developed all those many qualities which were demanded in a Hebrew king. During these days of training he had enjoyed rare opportunities for becoming acquainted with conditions within and about Israel. During his outlaw period he gathered about him a body of warriors who subsequently won for him his conquests. He appreciated, perhaps better than any one in his kingdom, the intensity of the rivalry between the tribes of Joseph and Judah. Consequently, although himself a Judean, he was able to soothe the bitter tribal jealousy, to overcome the instinct of separation which is naturally strong among Semitic peoples and had been intensified during the period of the judges, and to evolve out of the chaos a united Israel. Although the old rivalries frequently flamed into a passion, his wise and strong home-policy enabled him to hand over to his son an undivided kingdom. His able military policy extended the boundaries of the little Hebrew state until it included the small Canaanitish world which is bounded on the north by the Lebanons, on the east and south by the Arabian desert, and on the west by the coast plains. When he was called to the throne, the majority of the Israelites were vassals of the powerful Philistines; when he died, the Hebrew empire was recognized as paramount from the desert on the east to the great sea. It is not strange that later Hebrews idealized the character of David; they had every reason to regard him with pride and admiration. When we appreciate the limitations under which he accomplished his great achievements, we cannot hesitate to place him among the first conquerors and kings of antiquity.

139. DURING the latter days of David's rule the vitiating influence of Oriental ideas and customs became potent in the court at Jerusalem. The simplicity of the earlier days rapidly disappeared; the distance between the king and his subjects constantly increased. Broken by the effects of his own sins and those of his sons, David withdrew more and more into the seclusion of the harem. As growing infirmities caused him to relax his hold on affairs, the question of who should be the next king became important; the laws which were to determine the succession were still in the making. During the period of the judges, Gideon's shameless son Abimelech (sect. 56) had prepared his way to the throne of his father by the slaughter of his brothers. Saul's eldest son, Jonathan, seems to have been regarded as the prince regent; but death prevented his coming to the throne. In the subsequent history of David's family the eldest regularly succeeded, except in one or two cases, when he was inefficient. In the Semitic world the law of primogeniture was generally in force; among the Hebrews, however, the kingship was such a new institution that it was still elective, in the sense that the people claimed the right of accepting or rejecting a new candidate, even though he had been nominated by the preceding king. This fact

was demonstrated after the death of Solomon by the attitude of the northern tribes. David unfortunately, perhaps because of his infirmities, had not publicly nominated his successor. Conditions, therefore, in his court were peculiarly favorable for intrigue.

140. The oldest surviving prince was Adonijah, the son of Haggith. The prophetic historian states emphatically that " he was a very goodly man " (I. Kings i. 6), referring, probably, to his personal appearance. Being the eldest, he naturally aspired to the kingship. Following the example of his ill-fated brother Absalom, he assumed royal honors, preparing chariots, horsemen, and fifty runners to go before him when he appeared in public. The old king, although well aware of the significance of this act, gave no evidence of displeasure. The strength of Adonijah's claim was further established by the attitude of the stronger nobles of the realm; Joab, the old commander, Abiathar, the priest who had followed David during his outlaw days, and most of the princes espoused his cause. The ancient narrative gives only a few suggestions respecting the actual conditions within David's court.

It must have been clear to Adonijah that he had a formidable rival in Solomon, the son of the favorite Bathsheba. Zadok the priest and Nathan the prophet were the chief supporters of this younger aspirant. Apparently desiring to anticipate any sudden *coup d'état* which would place his rival on the throne, Adonijah invited his supporters and the leading nobles of the realm to a great feast at En-rogel, which may be identified with Job's well, located in the Kidron valley, a little to the south of Jerusalem. At a similar celebration at Hebron, Absalom had been proclaimed king. Furthermore, the conspicuous omission of Solomon and his partisans from the list of the invited guests was suspicious. Nathan, at once interpreting this act as a conspiracy to place Adonijah on the throne, hastened to inform Bathsheba that the son of her rival had been proclaimed king ; with the announcement, he proposed a plan whereby they might yet secure Solomon's succession. In accordance with his suggestion, Bathsheba gained an interview with the old king ; recalling his promise to her that her son should reign, she inquired how it was that Adonijah was already king. The announcement, which was calculated to arouse the resentment of a man who already felt the reins of power slipping from his nerveless grasp, was confirmed by Nathan, who came in according to arrangement while the queen was still with the king. The news of Adonijah's action and the artful words of the beautiful Bathsheba aroused David. First, he solemnly swore to her that her son should succeed him. Nathan, Zadok, and Benaiah, the commander of the royal body-guard, although belonging to the younger nobility, represented the religious and military classes of the kingdom. These supporters of Solomon, whom Adonijah to the wreck of his cause had left about the king, David, in order to carry his promises into immediate execution, summoned and commanded to place Solomon upon the royal mule, — thus announcing to the people that he had been chosen by the king as his successor; then, under the escort of the body-guard, they were to take him down to Gihon, which perhaps was that spring now known as the Virgin's Fount, situated a little above En-rogel. There Zadok and Nathan were to

anoint him king. These directions were immediately
carried out. After the anointing the trumpet was
blown, announcing that Solomon sat on the throne of
David. The people accepted him with loud acclama-
tions, crying, "God save King Solomon!" As the
crowd ascended to the upper city the sound of their
trumpets fell upon the ears of the banqueters who
were with Adonijah ; his question concerning the
cause of the uproar was speedily answered by a messenger, who announced that David had made Solomon
king, and that already the old monarch was receiving
the congratulations of the people over the accession of
his son.

141. The plan of Nathan and Bathsheba had succeeded. Solomon was master of the situation, for he
had not only the sanction and influence of the former
king, but also the support of the chief military force
in the empire, the six hundred. Adonijah's guests
fled to their homes, and he sought refuge at the altar,
fearing the sword of Solomon. But the new monarch's success was so complete that he could afford, for
the present at least, to refrain from bloodshed. Adonijah's pardon was granted, with the significant words :
"If he shall show himself a worthy man, there shall
not an hair of him fall to the earth ; but if wickedness be found in him, he shall die." Solomon received his obeisance, and curtly commanded, "Go to
thine house." His leniency was ominous.

Israel's new sovereign had good grounds to fear one
whose claims to the throne were so strong. Unfortunately for Adonijah, he soon aroused his brother's
suspicions. According to the record, he soon after
requested Bathsheba, who as the queen-mother was

recognized as one of the most influential in the state, to intercede with Solomon that he might give him as a wife the fair Shunamite who had cared for David during his last days. The request seemed so harmless that Bathsheba, prompted perhaps by the love of intrigue and matchmaking, consented. The petition, however, at once stirred up the king's wrath. According to Oriental ideas, the one who made the wives of a former king his own aspired to his regal power; this was the charge which Ishbaal brought against Abner (sect. 110), and in this manner Absalom publicly announced that he had mounted his father's throne (II. Sam. xvi. 22). Whether Adonijah's request was prompted by an ulterior design cannot be absolutely determined. Solomon's subsequent acts indicate that he was eager to remove all restraints upon his authority. He could never attain that absolutism which he craved while Adonijah and his sympathizers lived; consequently, he improved the opportunity to remove them at one blow. In the aspiring Benaiah, the head of the royal body-guard, he found a ready instrument. Adonijah, at Solomon's command, was slain without opportunity for defence. Nor was Adonijah the only victim. Joab's gray hairs, his patriotic services for Israel, and the sanctity of the altar to which he fled, did not save him. The life of Abiathar, the descendant of the priestly house of Eli, was spared because of his fidelity to David, and, probably, out of regard to his sacred office; he, however, was deposed and banished to his estate at Anathoth. The Benjaminite prince Shemei, who had betrayed his hostility to the Judean house of David on the occasion of Absalom's rebellion, was ordered never to leave the limits of

Jerusalem under penalty of death. Three years later he went to Gath in pursuit of one of his slaves who had fled thither; when he returned, Solomon mercilessly carried out his threat.

142. By these acts of bloodshed Solomon revealed his real character, and paved the way for that despotism which distinguished his reign. David had taken Bathsheba to his harem during the years of the war with the Ammonites, so that Solomon was not born until his father had reigned some time over all Israel; consequently, like Nero, he must have been young when the intrigues of his mother placed him upon the throne of Israel. That mother was Bathsheba, the one who had knowingly entered the harem of the murderer of her former husband; she imparted to Solomon her beauty, passion for show, love of power and unscrupulous methods. In the harem of David there was little to counteract and much to intensify this influence. With these facts in mind, it is easier to understand the Solomon of history than the inconsistent character to which we are introduced by later writers who in their religious teaching idealized the builder of their Temple (sect. 83). The influential members of his court also were those who had helped him to the throne, or who were ready to act subserviently to his will. Azariah the son of Nathan was one of his commanders, and another son, Zabud, bore the title of "king's friend." Zadok, of an unknown family, was placed in charge of the royal sanctuary to succeed the banished Abiathar. Benaiah, who had served him faithfully in removing his rivals and foes, was appointed to the command of the army. One of the sons of Zadok was a royal secretary; and another, who be-

came the king's son-in-law, had charge of the levies in
Naphtali.   Jehoshaphat, the Recorder, and Adoram,
who had charge of the levy, appear to have been the
only prominent officials under David who retained
their positions in the court of the new monarch.   It
was evident that the former traditions of the Hebrew
empire were being cast aside, and entirely different
principles were in the ascendency.

143. SOLOMON, reared in the enervating atmosphere
of an Oriental harem, had neither fondness nor apti-
tude for war. The unbroken peace which characterized his reign was due to the martial prestige inherited
from his father and his own disinclination to take up
the sword. In Edom the standard of revolt was raised
by a certain Hadad, who had escaped the general mas-
sacre of his kinsmen attendant upon their conquest by
Joab. At the Egyptian court, whither he sought refuge, he had been received favorably, and in time was
given a daughter of the reigning Pharaoh for wife.
When he heard of the death of David he forthwith
returned to rally his people; and among the rocky
fastnesses of Mount Seir they successfully defied the
son of their conqueror. A still more formidable rebellion broke out on the northeastern boundaries of Solomon's empire. It was headed by a Syrian, — Rezon,
the son of Eliada, a former dependant of Hadadezer,
that king of Zobah who figured in David's day as an
ally of the Ammonites, and subsequently as one of the
princes tributary to the Hebrews. Rezon, in time becoming master of Damascus, renounced the Israelitish
yoke. Being unmolested by Solomon, he was able to
lay the foundations of a powerful Syrian kingdom,

which was destined for generations to menace the independence of the Hebrews.

144. Instead of maintaining the supremacy of his nation by assuming the offensive, Solomon reversed the policy of his father and devoted the energies of his empire to strengthening its fortifications. His services in this direction certainly were most commendable. David had done little more than to fortify his capital city; but if the Israelites were to enjoy continued prosperity and freedom, their state must also be consolidated and provided with defences. At strategic points Solomon established fortified cities, equipped as arsenals, encircled with walls, and garrisoned with soldiers. Hazor protected the territory of Israel from attack on the north and northeast; Megiddo, on the southern side of the plain of Esdraelon, commanded the central parts of the land and the great highways which led up from the coast-plains to the west. Farther south, out on the borders of the Philistine plain, the Canaanitish town of Gezer, recently destroyed by the Egyptians and rebuilt by Solomon, guarded the western boundaries. Farther up among the hills of central Canaan was located the fortified town of Beth-horon, which commanded the passes leading from the lowlands to the neighborhood of Jerusalem. Baalath, whose exact site is unknown, was also similarly strengthened. The fortified town of Tamar, which was located on the southern limits of Canaan, out in the Judean desert (Ezek. xlvii. 19, xlviii. 28), furnished a defence against the incursions of desert robbers, and probably guarded the highway which led to the port of Ezion-geber on the arm of the Red Sea. The walls and fortifications of Jerusalem were also

extended and greatly strengthened, so that the humble city of David became a worthy capital of the Hebrew empire.

145. In his relations with the surrounding nations, Solomon's defensive policy was supplemented by diplomacy; what he could not win by arms he gained by intrigue. Alliances, far more than conquests, were conducive to the realization of his ambitions; accordingly, the friendly relations which had existed between Hiram of Tyre and David of Israel were cemented even more closely by his son. The Israelites had for barter the grain and wool which their trading neighbors needed; the Phœnicians, on the other hand, were in possession of the arts and products of that ancient civilization with which the Hebrews were still unfamiliar, and which were absolutely essential to the carrying out of Solomon's building enterprises, — consequently, the alliance was commercial in its nature and mutually profitable to both peoples. The greater advantage naturally accrued to the Israelitish king, for his wants were more imperative. The Hebrew historian also states that Hiram of Tyre was dissatisfied with the cities of western Galilee, which Solomon ceded to him in return for his services (I. Kings ix. 10–14). With the assistance of the artisans and sailors furnished by his Syrian ally, Solomon was able to build ships at Ezion-geber, on the Gulf of Akabah, and to send them out to engage in trade with the rich East. Setting sail from this southernmost point in the Hebrew empire, their course was along the shores of southern Arabia, which then enjoyed a high degree of prosperity and civilization; there they would find almost unlimited opportunities for barter. If Ophir is rightly identified

with Abhira at the mouth of the Indus,[1] they continued
their voyages even to India; the character of the products which they brought back, — ivory, apes, and peacocks, — and the foreign names which they applied to
them, tend to confirm this conjecture. Even with their
imperfect methods of navigation, it would be possible
to go and return from these distant ports within the
three years which was the time required for a voyage.
Such an extensive enterprise was in perfect keeping
with the spirit and aims of Solomon; and the Phœnician sailors on other seas demonstrated conclusively
their ability to carry it into execution.

146. Without much doubt, the aim of the visit of
the Queen of Sheba to Solomon was to establish a
commercial treaty between the two peoples whom they
represented; for Arabia, with its spices and precious
stones, had much to export which the Hebrews were
eager to secure. The stories which are recorded in
connection with this event are quite in keeping with
the practices of Oriental diplomacy. Alliances, sealed
with royal marriages, were made with other surrounding nations, including the Hittites, Moabites, Ammonites, and Edomites. To the minds of Solomon's
subjects the crowning glory of his reign was the marriage of their king to the daughter of Pasebchanu II.,
the last king of the twenty-first Egyptian dynasty.
This union with the venerable line of the Pharaohs
was most flattering to the vanity of a Canaanitish
prince whose father had been a humble shepherd; but
aside from the bride's dowry, which was the Canaanitish town of Gezer, it brought little lasting political
advantage to the Hebrews, for before Solomon's death

---

[1] See Christian Lassen: Indische Altertumskunde.

the throne of Egypt was seized by the Lybian usurper
Shishak. Even the alliance with Egypt had a commercial end. Solomon himself became a trader, and
exported thence great droves of horses, which he in
turn sold to his northern neighbors, the Syrians and
Hittites.

147. The effect of these close alliances with the
nations about, and of the extensive commerce which
sprang up as a result, was suddenly to introduce the
Israelites to the products and arts of the great Semitic
world about them. Hitherto struggles within and hostility without had rendered the Hebrew peasants almost
impervious to foreign influences; now, all at once, the
bars were thrown down, and these came rushing in
like a tidal wave. The horse took the place of the
ass; metal weapons and tools supplanted the rude
ones of flint and wood; walled cities arose on the
sites of the primitive towns with their mud and stone
hovels; the rude barracks of David grew into a palace; the simple gathering of followers about Saul, as
he sat under his tamarisk-tree in Ramah, developed
into a great Oriental court; luxuries undreamed of before came to be regarded as necessities; foreign spices,
apes, peacocks, ivory, precious stones and woods aroused
the curiosity and delighted the senses of the inhabitants
of the gay capital. With these radical changes in their
material surroundings came new customs, which tended
to modify materially their social life. The gods of a
Semitic nation were so thoroughly identified with the
state that an alliance between two peoples was regarded as an alliance between them also; consequently,
the toleration of the worship of the god or gods of each
ally within the territory of the other was at least postu-

lated.   In accordance with the terms of his alliances,
Solomon was therefore bound to rear temples for the
gods of his wives.   Thus the realization of his foreign
policy introduced grave religious dangers; while Jehovah was still universally regarded as the God of
Israel, he was being placed on the same plane with the
gods of the other nations.   Solomon, intent upon realizing his ideal of kingship, probably did not perceive
that the religion of Jehovah was menaced; in fact,
the danger was greater because so few recognized
its presence.   Certain enlightened prophets showed by
their subsequent action that they alone appreciated in
part, at least, the significance of the religious crisis
which was so apparent to later writers.

148. A study of his foreign policy has revealed the
dominating desires of Solomon.   They were to make
Israel like the nations about; to attain for himself the
absolute power of other Oriental monarchs, and to rival
them in the splendor and wealth of court and capital.
Totally disregarding those elements of originality which
gave the Hebrews their superiority over their neighbors, he sought only to level and imitate.   Much that
his policy brought to his people was good in itself, but
it was purchased at a great price.   His efforts being
chiefly directed toward gratifying his own love of dis-
play and luxury, his subjects, as a whole, suffered more
than they were benefited.   The royal estates were
widely extended, which meant that free land-holders
were deprived of their ancestral holdings, and in many
cases reduced to serfdom.   At Jerusalem he reared a
costly palace for himself; up among the Lebanons he
had another summer residence, whither he and his
court retired during the hot summer months.   The

court itself assumed a size and magnificence out of all proportion to the wealth and needs of the empire. Later historians have undoubtedly exaggerated the number of Solomon's wives: the Song of Songs speaks of only thirty queens and forty wives of the second rank (vi. 8); but the actual magnitude of his harem presented a glaring contrast to the simplicity of the preceding generation. Indeed, the institution itself was contrary to the higher ideals of the Hebrews, — as the teachings of the wise in their proverbs, and the practice of prophet and priest, demonstrate. It was introduced by David and Solomon, partially as a means of extending their influence, and partially in imitation of the Oriental potentates about them.

149. Although commerce and tribute must have brought to Solomon a large revenue, the chief expense of his luxurious court and extensive building enterprises necessarily rested upon the shoulders of his people. His palaces and citadels did not rise by magic nor with the aid of the jinns, as the naïve later traditions maintain. It was in keeping with his policy of Orientalism to reduce his subjects to serfdom. Up to this time the Canaanites, the ancient inhabitants of the land, had been allowed to dwell among the Hebrews, enjoying with them almost equal rights; in certain cases they even retained their own independent cities, — as, for example, Gibeon and Gezer. But under Solomon forced labor was imposed upon them, and that process of subjugation began which ultimately made them "hewers of wood and drawers of water." Nor were the Israelites themselves exempted. In accordance with the system in vogue in the East, the land was divided into twelve districts. In this divi-

sion the tribal boundaries were purposely disregarded; Judah alone is not mentioned, suggesting that Solomon favored his own tribe. Over these districts were placed royal officers, whose duty was to collect taxes for the support of the court. Probably, also, under their direction were raised the great levies of men through whose labors Solomon's huge building projects were carried into execution. The later prophetic historian, who penned the eighth chapter of I. Samuel (sect. 75), undoubtedly had clearly in mind the condition of the Israelites under their grand monarch when he represented the old seer as declaring: " He will take your sons and appoint them unto him for his chariots and to be his horsemen, and they shall run before his chariots; and he will appoint them unto him for captains of thousands, and captains of fifties; and some to plough his ground and to reap his harvest, and to make his instruments of war and the equipment of his chariots. And he will take your daughters to be perfumers and cooks and bakers. And he will take your fields and your vineyards and your oliveyards, even the best of them, and give them to his servants; and he will take the tenth of your seed and of your vineyards, and give them to his officers and to his servants. And he will take your menservants and your maidservants, and your goodliest young men, and your asses, and put them to work. He will take the tenth of your flocks; and ye shall be his servants."

150. The free-born Israelites soon learned by bitter experience the cost of all the show, glitter, pomp, and splendor which dazzled them for a time, and rendered the reign of Solomon so glorious in the eyes of later generations. Undoubtedly, many a passionate cry for

number of proverbial sayings and songs. Like the later wise, he employed many comparisons drawn from Nature, — fables concerning the trees, beasts, and fishes, to impress and illustrate his brilliant deductions. This kind of wit is peculiarly acceptable to the Oriental mind. When it fell from the lips of such a king as Solomon, there is little wonder that many came from afar to listen to and enjoy the luxuriance of his court. Long after, when posterity had forgotten his follies, his sage maxims were cherished, and his reputation as the father of wisdom-thought steadily grew. In the succeeding centuries, proverbs of unknown authorship coming from an earlier period were naturally attributed to him. Since a proverb voices the common experience of humanity, it is obvious that the name of the one who first gave it definite expression, if known at first, is quickly forgotten; consequently, the collection of maxims which bore the general title "Proverbs of Solomon" rapidly increased in size. This point is well illustrated by the Book of Proverbs. Its general superscription suggests that the entire anthology came from the son of David; but a further investigation demonstrates, that, according to the testimony of the book itself, a large part came from other wise men. Chapter xxii. 17 introduces a small group of maxims which are designated as the "words of the wise," and a still shorter collection "also from the wise" is preserved in xxiv. 23–34. In chapter xxx. "the words of Agur," and in chapter xxxi. "the words of King Lemuel," are found. A study of the contents of chapters i.–ix. reveals the fact that they consist of a general commendation of wisdom, probably written by a later editor as an introduction to the collection contained in x. 1–xxii.

16, which bears the title, "The Proverbs of Solomon."
Consequently, only the two larger sections of the book
— x. 1–xxii. 16 and xxviii.–xxix. — are definitely assigned to Solomon.   When among these are found
pictures of a ruler just and considerate of the interests
of his people, — the antithesis of the Solomon of history, — and proverbs commending monogamy and fru-
gality, and religious maxims infused with the spirit of
genuine piety, the conviction grows that a large proportion of the proverbs in these collections could never
have come from Solomon.   The titles, therefore, must
be regarded as characteristically concrete Hebrew ex-
pressions for "Proverbs of Antiquity."   This inference
is confirmed by the observation that most of them are
written, not from the point of view of a king, but of a
subject belonging to the middle class; consequently,
they represent the combined wisdom of many different wise men living during the centuries following
Solomon.   That some of the three thousand proverbs
which the great king is reputed to have spoken are
preserved in these anthologies is exceedingly probable,
although it is far easier to indicate with certainty those
which are not rather than those which are from him.
The same tendency to attribute all wisdom-writings to
Solomon explains the title of the late book of Ecclesiastes, "The words of Koheleth, the son of David, king
in Jerusalem."   Similarly, an apocryphal writer enti-
tled his book "The Wisdom of Solomon."

153. The further idealization of the character and
reign of Solomon may be followed in later tradition.
The broader and deeper elements which have gradually
come to be associated with the adjective "wise" have
been attributed by succeeding generations to that one

who was wise only according to the imperfect standards of his age. In organizing the empire, and in inaugurating a more perfect system of civil tribunals, Solomon proved himself wise in the highest sense; but in adopting the policy of the Oriental rulers about him, he deliberately turned his back upon the higher ideals of his race. Saul, with all his defects, was a far nobler man and a truer patriot. Solomon forgot the best interests of his people in the pursuit of luxury and splendor. In realizing his ambition he nearly wrecked his nation. The little state which his son inherited maintained a struggling existence for a few centuries; while the northern kingdom, battling against greater odds, soon went down to its ruin.

XIII

154. THE favor which Solomon enjoyed in the eyes of later generations of Jews grew because they recognized in him the builder of the sanctuary about which their national faith centred. It is exceedingly improbable, however, that the founder of the Temple appreciated the real significance of his action. He may even have regarded the temple which he reared as only one of the more important of the collection of buildings which together constituted the royal palace. Its size and magnificence were tangible proofs of the gratitude which he and his father felt toward Jehovah for the victories and prosperity which he had given them. Being the royal shrine, it was in a sense from the first a national sanctuary; but the idea of its entirely supplanting all others did not arise until centuries later, as the study of the subsequent history will demonstrate. Even in building the Temple, Solomon was emulating the example of the Oriental kings about him. Hiram of Tyre readily understood his desire, and rendered most valuable assistance. Solomon's subjects were entirely ignorant of the higher arts which were so essential to palace building. Tyrian artisans taught and aided the Israelites, who, under Solomon's rule, became a nation of toilers. Upon the heights of Lebanon cedars and cypresses were cut

189

down; with great labor their trunks were transported by land and sea to Joppa, thence to the city of David, thirty-five miles up over the Judean hills. The limestone ledge upon which the town was built was quarried, furnishing the material for foundation and walls.

155. The palace and Temple were located on the narrow ridge of rock running north and south, which was bounded on the east by the Kidron, and on the west by the Tyropœan valley. Its natural strength and the presence of a spring on its southern slope had led the Jebusites to build their citadel upon it (sect. 114). In the Old Testament books which were written while the palace and Temple were still standing, there occur many references to going up from the palace to the Temple, or from the latter down to the king's house (I. Kings viii. 1. II. Kings xi. 19. Jer. xxii. 1; xxvi. 10; xxxvi. 9–12). Since the palace was lower than the Temple, it is clear that it could not have been located on the traditional Mount Zion, to the southwest, for this is far higher than the highest point of Mount Moriah on which Solomon's buildings stood. The same references indicate that the site of the Temple must be sought above that of the palace. Israelitish as well as Canaanitish shrines in that age were located on the high places. The evidence, therefore, points to the highest rock on Mount Moriah, which is to-day crowned by the Mohammedan shrine known as the "Dome of the Rock." A fountain, connected with underground water-conduits, also marks the spot, and in antiquity probably furnished the water for purification which was so necessary in connection with the sacrifice. Tradition also marks this as the sacred spot; and its testimony is here valuable, because there is

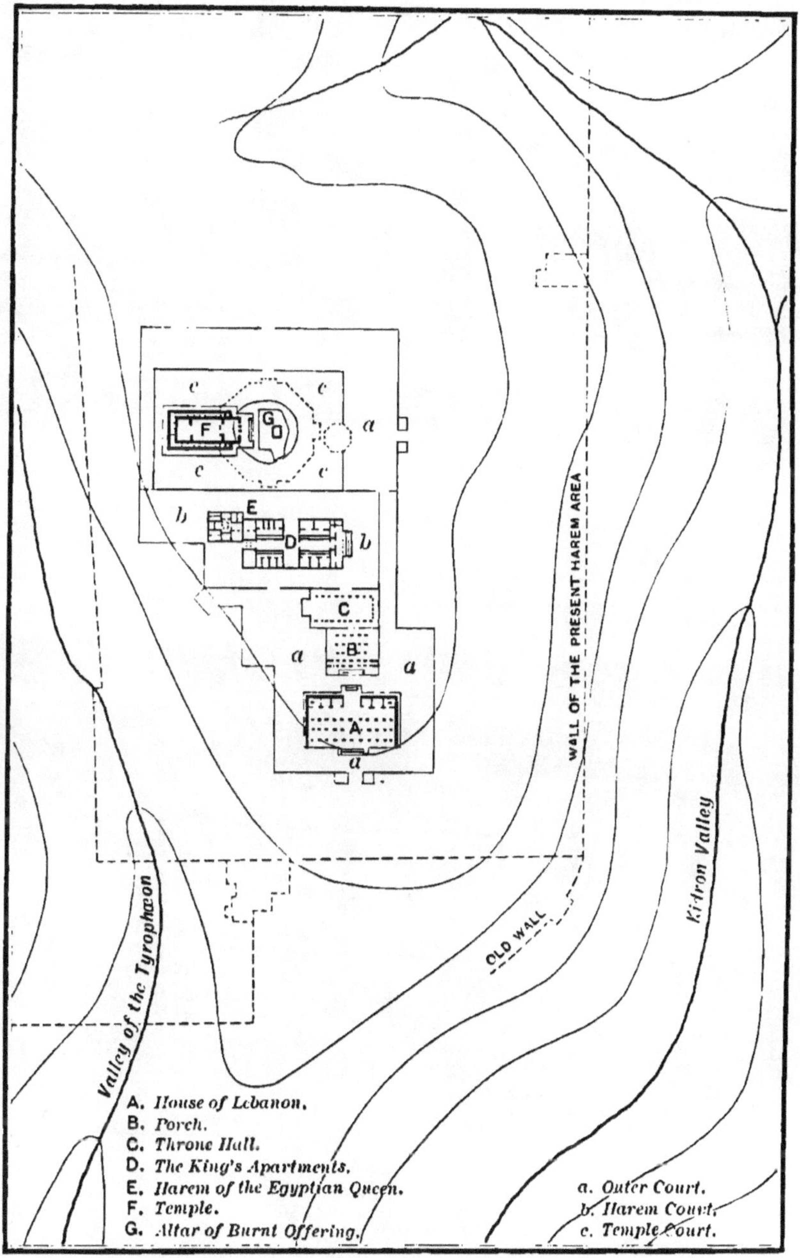

c
c
F
G
a
c
c
b
E
D
b
C
a
B
a
A
a
WALL OF THE PRESENT HAREM AREA
OLD WALL
Kidron Valley
Valley of the Tyrophœon
A. House of Lebanon.
B. Porch.
C. Throne Hall.
D. The King's Apartments.
E. Harem of the Egyptian Queen.
F. Temple.
G. Altar of Burnt Offering.
a. Outer Court.
b. Harem Court.
c. Temple Court.

PLAN OF SOLOMON'S PALACE

(ACCORDING TO STADE)

little doubt that this was the site of Herod's temple,
which was built in place of the humble one reared by
the exiles who returned from Babylon. The period of
the captivity was so brief that those who rebuilt the
Temple would have little difficulty in finding the old
site. Furthermore, the configuration of the rock at
this point alone fulfils the conditions. Inasmuch as
the Temple faced the east, it must have extended
westward from the rock; while on the eastern side of
the area was found the entrance to the sanctuary, the
great bronze altar, and the open court. Close to the
Temple and a little to the southeast, as the configuration of the rock made necessary, were located the
other buildings of the palace. The present harem
area was amply sufficient to accommodate all these
and their encircling courts.

156. On approaching the palace from the south, the
first edifice was the House of Lebanon, — so called
because its upper stones rested upon forty-five pillars,
arranged in three rows of fifteen, made from the costly
cedars of Lebanon. Its dimensions were one hundred
cubits long, fifty cubits broad, and thirty high. The
cubit in use at this time was probably the king's cubit
(see Ezekiel xliii. 13), corresponding to the larger old
Egyptian cubit, which was equal to $20\frac{3}{4}$ inches.[1] Its
dimensions in round numbers therefore would be one
hundred and seventy-five feet long, eighty-five feet
wide, and fifty feet high. The lower story, which was
open and well lighted, furnished a large audience-
room for public assemblies; the references suggest
that the chambers above were used for storing weapons and military equipment (I. Kings x. 16, 17;

[1] See Nowack: Lehrbuch der Hebräischen Archäologie, i. 199–201.

Isaiah xxii. 8). Beyond the House of Lebanon were two halls. The first, which was about eighty-five feet in length and fifty in breadth, was a large porch with numerous pillars, and was open on one side at least; the second was probably joined directly to the first, and enclosed with cedar. There Solomon's throne of judgment was set up, and thither the people brought their cases before the supreme tribunal of the kingdom. The first hall may have served as a waiting-room for the petitioners for justice. Between these public buildings and the Temple were located the private apartments of the king, with adjoining quarters for his Egyptian queen. These structures, like the Judgment Hall, were made of hewn stone and finished with cedar. This series of royal buildings was similar in many ways to the palaces of contemporary Oriental monarchs. It is also significant that thirteen years were devoted to their building, while the Temple required but seven.

157. For our knowledge of the details of the Temple we are in part indebted to Ezekiel, the prophet-priest who had himself served in the old sanctuary before he was carried away into exile. His visions, therefore, of the new Temple which was to be reared, were largely suggested by his memories of the old. Of the many who have written upon Solomon's Temple, Professor Stade has made the most careful analysis of the sources,[1] and later investigations have tended to confirm rather than modify his conclusions. Although many questions of detail are answered only by later traditions, which in most cases are misleading, the general outlines of the Temple are distinctly drawn

[1] Geschichte des Volkes Israel, i. 326–343.

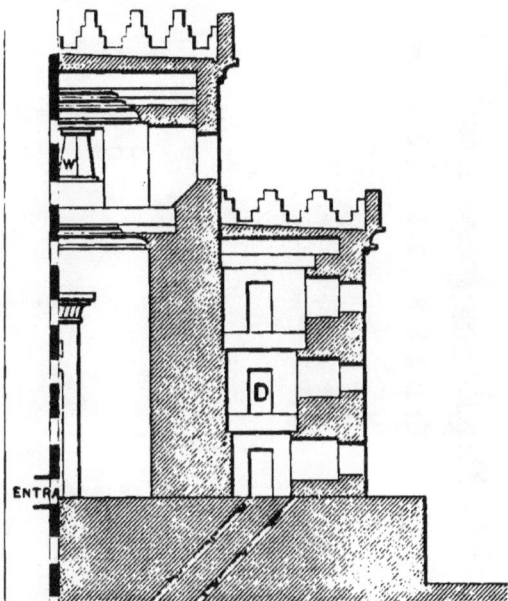

D

ENTR

TION.

30   40   50 CUBITS.
        10   20 METERS.

W. *Windows.*
nber.   *a. Altar.*
        e. Entrance to Side Chambers.

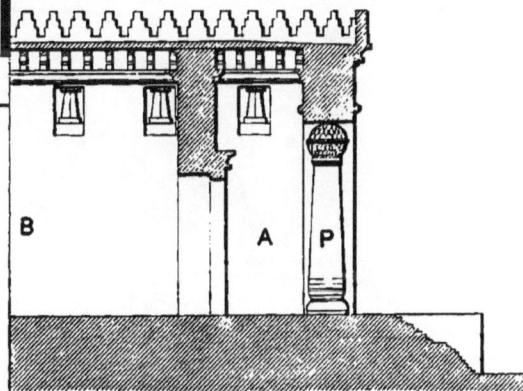

B   A   P

AL SECTION.

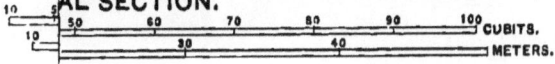

10   5
        50   60   70   80   90   100 CUBITS.
10
                        30   40   METERS.

LE.

H. S. MABIE, DEL.

GROUND PLAN

CROSS SECTION

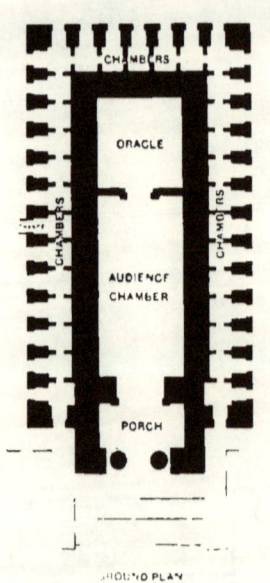

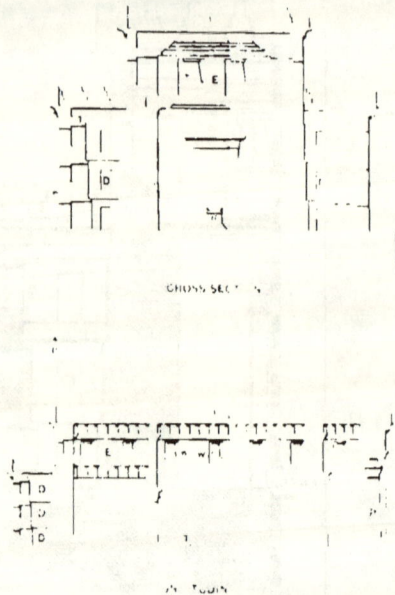

RESTORATION OF SOLOMON'S TEMPLE.
ACCORDING TO STADE

in the old stratum of narrative in I. Kings. At
the western end of the sacred structure was a cu-
bical enclosure about thirty-five feet square; this
was the heart of the Temple, for it was set apart as
the dwelling-place of Jehovah, and was known as the
Oracle. By later generations it was appropriately
called the Holy of Holies. The Ark, the symbol of
Jehovah's presence, was placed in the centre; and
on either side, towering seventeen feet high, stood the
cherubim, made of olive-wood and overlaid with gold.
Their outstretched wings were each about nine feet in
width, and touched the wall on either side, meeting in
the centre over the Ark; in form and significance they
probably corresponded to the great colossi — with the
body of an ox, the face of a man, and the wings of an
eagle — which guarded the entrances to the ancient
Assyrian palaces. The general plan of the Temple
made no arrangements for lighting the Oracle, and the
references to Jehovah "who dwelleth in thick darkness" (I. Kings viii. 12) suggest that it was lighted
only as the olive-wood doors were opened which led
into the larger room in front. The latter corresponded
to an audience-chamber in the palace of an earthly
king; it was of the same width as the Oracle, but
about fifty feet in height and seventy feet in length.
The walls of the Temple were of hewn stone, and according to Ezekiel about ten feet in thickness on the
ground (Ezek. xli. 5), and on the outside a cubic less
for each higher story. The walls on the interior were
ceiled with boards of cedar, so that they were completely covered; elaborate mural decorations gave
them an added splendor. The floors were of cypress-
wood. Light was admitted into the outer sanctuary

by windows on both sides, placed close up under the
ceiling; the roof was probably flat, and projected so
as to keep the rain from beating in through these ap-
ertures. Immediately in front of the entrance to the
Oracle stood the little altar of cedar-wood, on which
was placed the shewbread. Great square doors, with
olive-wood posts and cypress panels, led from the
large audience-room to the porch, which was of the
same width as the Temple, and about sixteen feet in
length. At the entrance stood two huge, hollow
bronze pillars about thirty feet high and nearly six
feet in diameter (Jer. lii. 21); these were decorated
with bronze work, representing pomegranates and
lilies; they were probably associated with the symbolism of the Temple, possibly being related to the pillars
which once stood beside the altars of Jehovah.

158. Immediately in front of the Temple, which
faced the east, was placed the large bronze altar which
was used for the sacrifices; part, if not all of it, probably rested on the broad rock which still crowns the
Temple mount. Near by, to supply the water needful
for purification, stood the great brazen sea, which was
nearly nine feet high and over fifty feet in circumfer-
ence; it was supported by twelve bronze oxen. On
three sides of the Temple were built a series of chambers, three stories in height, extending up to the high
windows which lighted the sanctuary; their outer walls
probably corresponded on the inside (sect. 157) to the
peculiar pyramid-like exterior walls of the Temple, so
that the rooms in the lower stories would be much
smaller than those in the upper (see drawings). The
entrance to these chambers was from the south side.
Stairs led up from the lower to the higher rooms, which

were used for storing the wardrobes of the priests and
the vessels employed in the ritualistic service. The
Temple probably stood on a raised platform similar to
that upon which the Dome of the Rock now stands,
and was surrounded by an open court, encircled by a
wall of hewn stone covered by cedar timbers.

159. The architectural design and details of the
Temple of Solomon have been identified in turn with
Egyptian, Syrian, and Babylonian models. The variety
of opinion may be explained by the fact that all these
types had certain general characteristics in common.
The Phœnicians who planned and directed the building of Solomon's sanctuary were in close touch with
these peoples, and as was their wont undoubtedly
adopted ideas from each. The Syrian models, however, were followed most closely. In facing toward the
rising sun, it shared the characteristic of every Baal
temple. It is distinctly stated that all the metal work,
including the making of the lavers and the utensils for
the sacrificial service, was under the direction of a certain Hiram, or Huram, the son of a famous Tyrian
worker in metals (II. Chron. ii. 14). Cherubim, pillars, bronze altars, brazen sea, and bronze vessels were
all in use in connection with Phœnician temples, while
the lily and palm-branch frequently appear on their inscriptions. Even in the ritual which gradually grew
up about the Temple, it is difficult to select any one
custom which did not have its analogy among some
contemporary Semitic people. The potency of the influence which the Temple exercised upon the religious
development of the Hebrews and of humanity was the
result, not of its form nor of its magnificence nor of its
ritual, but simply of the character of the unseen God
to whom it was dedicated.

SOCIAL AND RELIGIOUS CONDITIONS UNDER THE
UNITED KINGDOM

160. THE century which intervened between the
accession of Saul and the death of Solomon was one
of unparalleled development for the Israelites. Within
three generations the Hebrew kingdom had been born,
reached its zenith, and begun to decline. The social
transformations were correspondingly rapid. The
establishment of the kingdom crystallized the latent
tendencies of the period of the judges. The disintegration of the tribal organization, which had already
begun under the combined influence of intermarriage,
the growth of cities, and common danger, was accel-
erated. When the Hebrews came to fight together
under a common leader for a common cause, national
loyalty took the place of a narrow tribal loyalty. In
the earlier days the supreme power had been vested in
the heads of the tribes; under the kingdom, however,
it was in the hands of the king. About him grew up
a new nobility, who soon almost completely usurped
the authority of the tribal elders. Under Saul and
David the chief peers of the realm were the relatives
of the reigning monarch and his most prominent military leaders. In accordance with his policy of Orientalism, the nobles of Solomon's court were either
immediate members of his own family, or those personally dependent upon him for their position. The

old assembly of the elders of the tribes fell into dis-
use, and as a consequence their power waned. Solomon struck an open and effective blow against the old
tribal organization when, ignoring the ancient boundaries, he divided the territory of Israel into twelve
districts, classing together people from different tribes
and clans.

161. Under the kingdom, the lot of the individual
was also materially altered. Before this time he had
been responsible to almost no authority, but it was
a freedom begotten by a state of anarchy ; the weaker,
as a result, was the slave of the stronger. The bur-
den of a foreign yoke made it an odious bondage; consequently, the establishment of the kingship brought
real independence to the individual. Originally the
Hebrew king was only a judge whose authority had
become hereditary ; his relation to the nation corresponded to that of the chief to his tribe, or that of the
modern sheik to his clan ; he was their leader in war,
their counsellor and judge in time of peace ; in the
truest sense, therefore, he was the servant of the people
who had called him to be their head. In reality the
Hebrew state was a democracy, and so it remained
under Saul ; during a period of peace he returned to
his own estate, where he lived with a few followers
about him. The chief obligations of the people to
their king were to rally around him for battle in a
time of common danger. Hence, under Israel's first
king the people enjoyed the most perfect freedom and
equality. These conditions continued during David's
reign, because the rich tribute which poured in from
his conquests supplied the increased needs of his growing court. Solomon, however, completely reversing

the original Hebrew idea of a king, proceeded on the assumption that the people were his servants. To be sure, the new régime afforded additional security to the individual, and introduced him to a higher material civilization; but the form of the introduction was so painful that it made little lasting impression. Meantime he was deprived of his old independence; his lands, wealth, family, and person were treated as the possessions of the monarch. His enslavement was rendered none the easier to bear by the striking contrast — which he could not fail to observe — between the want and poverty of his home and the magnificence of Solomon's capital and court; nor could he forget that this was purchased at the cost of his own freedom. For the private citizen the dissolution of the empire afforded a most welcome relief, since it restored the simpler conditions of the earlier days, under which he regained in part his old rights and independence.

162. The inauguration of the kingdom did not sweep away all the moral darkness of the preceding period. Enemies were still tortured, the truth was held none too sacred, women were not exempted from the cruelties of war, and polygamy was exceedingly common. Nevertheless, there was also tangible evidence of advancement. When a stable government was established, the rights of life and property were more clearly defined and more carefully regarded. In this age the stealing of the priest of Micah by the Danites (sect. 69) would have been summarily punished; Gideon's slaughter of the elders of Succoth and Penuel (sect. 66) would also have aroused a thrill of horror. Adultery was recognized as a crime. Even the weak could hope for justice before such judges as

David and Solomon. The law of blood-revenge was still in vogue, but it was gradually being superseded by trial before an authorized tribunal. A friendship such as was that between David and Jonathan, and gratitude like that of the people of Jabesh-Gilead, lighted up the moral darkness. In every department of life the rudeness of barbarism was giving place to the amenities of civilization and the influence of a higher conception of the demands of Jehovah.

The religious life of the Israelites was also deeply affected by this new step forward. The external religious forms which had been so heterogeneous in different parts of the land became uniform in proportion as the political organization of the nation became more complete. The people still worshipped at many different shrines, scattered throughout the land, but the royal sanctuary at Jerusalem enjoyed a peculiar prestige; being free from old traditions and customs, its service was naturally purer. On occasions sacrifice was offered by any one, irrespective of priestly calling. The townsmen of Ramah sacrificed on their high place (I. Sam. ix. 13). Samuel, the Ephraimitish seer, frequently attended to this function. When he brought the Ark to Jerusalem David danced before it, clad in the linen garment of a priest (II. Sam. vi. 14). Soon after his accession Solomon sacrificed a thousand burnt-offerings on the great altar at Gibeon (I. Kings iii. 4); at the consecration of the Temple he officiated at the sacrifice, performing his royal duties as the priest of his nation (I. Kings viii. 22, 62–65). "Three times a year did Solomon offer burnt-offerings and peace-offerings upon the altar which he built unto the Lord" (I. Kings ix. 25). At the same time the num-

bers of the regularly appointed priests increased, and
their functions became more clearly defined.   When
the sanctuary at Shiloh was destroyed, the descendants
of Eli the priest migrated to Nob, a little to the north
of Jebus ; there they remained until Saul, in a fit of
madness, caused them to be slain because they had
hospitably received the outlaw David (sect. 97).
Abiathar, who escaped, followed David in his fortunes,
and ultimately was placed in charge of the royal sanctuary at Jerusalem ; his attachment to the cause of
Adonijah, however, cost him his position soon after the
accession of Solomon, and his colleague, Zadok, a
priest of unknown family, was appointed in his place ;
the descendants of Zadok continued as guardians of
the Temple until the fall of Jerusalem.   Other royal
priests are mentioned.   Ira, the Jairite, served in conjunction with Abiathar and Zadok (II. Sam. xx. 25).
Certain of David's sons were priests (II. Sam. viii. 18).
Under Solomon, Azariah, a son of his favorite noble, —
the prophet Nathan, — was also elected to the priesthood (I. Kings iv. 5).   These references indicate that
the priests of the royal sanctuary, at least, were appointed at the will of the king, and being regarded
as regular officers of the court, were dependent upon
the reigning sovereign.   As they were the avowed
champions of form and precedent, they proved most
stable supporters of the monarchy.   The usage of the
royal sanctuary indicates that son succeeded father in
taking charge of a public shrine ; so that the priesthood, like the kingship, in time became hereditary.

163.   The chief functions of the priest appear at first
to have been to determine the will of Jehovah.   The
Danite spies, for example, consulted the priest of Micah

to ascertain whether they should be prospered in their search for a new home, and gained a favorable response (Judges xviii. 5, 6). Saul hastened to consult the oracle through Ahijah, his priest, before following the fleeing Philistines who had been put to flight by Jonathan's prowess; the evidence of the general rout, however, was soon so conclusive that the impulsive king did not await further confirmation (I. Sam. xiv. 18–20). David, during his outlaw days, never took an important step without consulting the oracle of Jehovah (I. Sam. xxiii. 2; II. Sam. ii. 1).

The exact manner in which the priest determined the divine will is not indicated. The sacred lot was in common use at this period. In the illustrations cited, the questions asked were capable of either a negative or an affirmative answer. In the light of these facts it is not improbable that Jehovah was consulted by a form of lot, rendered peculiarly sacred because presided over by the priest and cast before some symbol of the Deity as the Ark or an ephod. Like most of the external religious practices of the Hebrews at this time, it had its analogy among other Semitic nations.

164. The additional duties of the priest were more perfunctory. Since they were the custodians of the Temple and of local shrines and their treasures, the ceremonies connected with sacrifice were by degrees confided to their keeping, until at a later time no one else was allowed to perform them. The examples which have been cited are sufficient to demonstrate conclusively that the custom was now only in the making. At this time, however, the standing and functions of the priests gave them a position of commanding influence. They were the revered counsellors of king

and people; by all they were recognized as the minis-
ters of Jehovah. Sometimes, doubtless by words, but
more often by religious symbolism, they impressed
upon the mind of the Israelites the great truths which
were the possession of the Hebrew race at that stage in
their development. Since at this time public annals
began to be kept, and certain song-books like "The
Wars of Jehovah" and "The Book of the Upright"
were in existence, it is not improbable that the more
common laws were also being committed to writing.

165. Among the Arabs, the prophet bore a name
corresponding to the Hebrew designation for priest.
In the earlier days of Hebrew history the functions of
the priest and seer were only imperfectly differentiated.
Samuel, the seer, performed the rite of sacrifice, and
the son of Nathan the prophet was a royal priest. To
ascertain the will of Jehovah one resorted either to the
seer or the priest. This fact is clearly stated in a passage referring to Israel's first king: " And when Saul
inquired of the Lord, the Lord answered him not,
neither by dreams, nor by Urim, nor by prophets "
(I. Sam. xxviii. 6). The Hebrew prophets at first,
therefore, were properly seers; the passage in I. Samuel ix. 9 confirms this conclusion, distinctly stating that
"he that is now called a Prophet was beforetime called
a Seer." The seers were in turn distinct from the sons
of the prophets, to whom reference is first made during
the days of Saul. The latter, living together in guilds,
usually in connection with some sanctuary, seem to
have corresponded in Hebrew life to the Baal prophets
of Phœnicia. They were religious enthusiasts, who
gave expression to their emotions by throwing themselves into a wild ecstatic state, — sometimes by the

aid of artificial means (I. Sam. x. 5–7; xix. 20–24), as did the prophets of Baal on Mount Carmel (I. Kings xviii. 26, 28). While they were an unmistakable index of the intensity of the faith of Israel, and must have kindled the religious and patriotic feelings of their countrymen, yet the designation "prophet" in the peculiar sense in which it came to be used among the Hebrews cannot properly be applied to them.

166. The character and work of certain of the Hebrew seers during this period indicate that the later conception of a Jehovah-prophet was beginning to unfold (sect. 5). Samuel ceased to be a mere seer when he found Saul and inspired him to the act which placed him on the throne; although the records are late, they suggest that he also figured prominently in the subsequent history of the nation. Nathan certainly was less a seer than a statesman. The one recorded message of the royal seer, Gad, was concerning a question of national interest (II. Sam. xxiv.). Solomon, while favoring the priests, appears to have ignored the seers. The eleventh and twelfth chapters of I. Kings contain references which show that they opposed his Orientalism in a manner very similar to that of later prophets like Amos and Isaiah, who courageously fought the same evil.

The term "prophet" may with reason, therefore, be applied to certain men who stood forth prominently during the days of the united monarchy to interpret the will of Jehovah concerning the political, social, and religious questions of their age.

167. At the same time it is manifest that the most enlightened Hebrews still conceived of Jehovah very imperfectly. Michal, the daughter of Saul and wife

of David, had a teraphim, or family idol, in her house
(I. Sam. xix. 13). The Temple itself, with its brazen
oxen and cherubim, contained much which recalled the
current Canaanitish symbolism. Jehovah was not yet
regarded as the God of the universe, but only of the
land and people of Israel. Even David is represented
as complaining, when hunted by Saul, "They have
driven me out this day that I should not cleave unto
the inheritance of the Lord, saying, ' Go, serve other
gods ' " (I. Sam. xxvi. 19). Solomon reared temples
to the gods of the allied nations. When king and
people united in offering innocent human beings as a
sacrifice to appease Jehovah, and left their bodies a
prey to beast and bird (II. Sam. xxi.), it is evident that
their knowledge of him was still very incomplete;
they even thought of him as becoming angry with his
people, and for no apparent reason leading David
on to a deed of folly, which was in turn punished by
a grievous pestilence (II. Sam. xxiv.).

The Hebrew ideas respecting the life after death
were as indefinite as among other early nations.
When men died, they were thought of as sleeping
with their fathers in Sheol, the abode of shades,
whence there was no return (I. Kings ii. 10; II.
Sam. xii. 23). The belief that the spirits of those
whose bodies were left unburied were peculiarly un-
happy, probably explains the heroic conduct of Rizpah
in watching over the bodies of her sons (II. Sam.
xxi.), and the action of the people of Jabesh-gilead
in burying the bodies of Saul and Jonathan (I. Sam.
xxxi.).

168. Meantime there was progress. The basis of
morality among the Israelites was their conception of

Jehovah. When they did wrong, they felt that they had sinned against him; and if punishment came, it was from their God. Consequently, the remarkable advance in ethical standards which appeared under the kingdom is the best possible proof that the Israelites conceived of Jehovah ever more definitely as a God who demanded righteousness in his people because he himself was righteous.

The establishment of an independent Hebrew state led them to recall their past history, and especially the teachings of their great leader Moses, who had led them to the land of their abode. In a sense, therefore, it represented a renaissance of Mosaism. Ideas which had suffered eclipse during the unsettled period of the judges again came to the ascendancy, just as the Ark again came into prominence. It has already been noted (sect. 71) that the idea of Jehovah's unity was inseparably connected with that of the unity of his people. The union of all the tribes under one human king, by a simple analogy, intensified their faith in one Divine King, and counteracted in a most effectual manner the temptations which persistently beset them to worship the local Canaanitish deities. Since their thought was always concrete, this new conception of a king represented an important advance in their idea of Jehovah; it included their former concepts of counsellor, deliverer, and judge, and added those of majesty and supreme power. When success rewarded their struggles for independence, they were impressed again by the old truth which had been often illustrated in their history, that Jehovah was able and willing to deliver them; when their armies met those of other nations, Jehovah demonstrated conclusively to their minds by every victory that he was superior to the gods of these other peoples. Consequently, as never before, the hearts of the Israelites were filled with an unbounded admiration and gratitude toward Jehovah. The atmosphere was favorable for the growth of popular faith; storms were destined to come which would deepen and broaden it, but from Dan to Beersheba the God of their nation was fervently worshipped by every loyal Israelite.

In this earlier period, half enveloped in the mists of heathenism, filled with deeds of rude barbarism, stupendous folly, heroic struggles, and glorious conquests, the roots of later Hebrew life and thought are found firmly embedded. The conquests of David and the glory of Solomon also gave Jehovah a prestige and place among the nations which further crystallized the faith of his people. Amidst the vicissitudes and misfortunes of succeeding years it was kept alive and strengthened by the memories of this golden epoch. When their enlightened prophets beheld afar the splendors of a more glorious day, they drew the language and figures wherewith they heralded it from the annals of the united monarchy. David, who was its central figure, became the type of the Lord's anointed, who was coming to bring lasting deliverance, peace, and joy to his people, — not by the sword, but by the far more potent power of divine truth.

APPENDIX

THE AUTHORITIES UPON HEBREW HISTORY

APPENDIX

THE AUTHORITIES UPON HEBREW HISTORY

In the modern study of history a library is the only satisfactory text-book. This is peculiarly true of Hebrew history, where the facts must be gleaned from many different sources. To-day, when the number of books on biblical and related subjects is so great, the question which the student constantly asks is, not what are helpful, but rather what books are the most helpful and trustworthy. In the following pages the attempt is made to answer this question definitely and practically. Under the chapter headings employed in the *History* the biblical passages, which are our first and great source, are systematically arranged. Then follow page references to the writers who have thrown the clearest light upon the subjects treated. Primary rather than secondary authorities are in most cases cited. For the convenience of those unfamiliar with the German, the references to the English books are introduced first. The explanation of the abbreviations adopted will be found on page 213, where the books of reference are arranged under their respective heads.

With many of these works the reader is already familiar. Nevertheless, a very brief characterization may be found helpful to some.

Of the many books in English which treat of the authorship, date, and contents of the Old Testament writings, none present the results of recent critical research in more concise and usable form than the *Introduction*, by Professor Driver. For the student who will familiarize himself with the technical terms employed, and faithfully look up the

14

biblical references with which the volume is filled, it is an invaluable manual.   Professor Moore's commentary on *Judges* presents in greater detail the latest critical conclusions concerning this important source of Hebrew history. The data respecting the social and religious life of the Israelites during the period of the judges are especially valuable. Although Wellhausen's *Prolegomena to the History of Israel* has aroused bitter antagonism, largely because of its tone, and although some of its conclusions are too extreme to do justice to all the facts, it must be recognized as an epoch-making book, and one which still amply rewards patient study.

In his *Aids to the Devout Study of Criticism*, Professor Cheyne outlines in a half-popular manner an analysis of the David-narratives in Samuel, and then introduces the reader to the David of the old records.   General questions concerning the origin and aim of the Old Testament books and the practical results of the historical and literary study of the Bible are ably discussed by Professor Horton in his *Revelation and the Bible*.   In the *Wise Men of Ancient Israel and their Proverbs* the present writer, after studying the three great classes of Hebrew teachers, investigates the question of the date and authorship of the Book of Proverbs, and then rearranges the contents of the Hebrew anthology.

Professor Budde's exhaustive analysis of *Die Bücher Richter und Samuel* has justly become the foundation for all subsequent critical study of their structure and authorship.   Among the many German *Einleitungen in das Alte Testament*, that of Professor Cornill is especially serviceable, since it is concise as well as critical.

In the department of Hebrew history there is a remarkable lack of works in English written with the historical spirit.   Those of Edersheim and Smith are based upon the old traditional view of the sources.   The same objection is only partially true in the case of Stanley's *History of the*

Jewish Church, which is still very useful in connection with certain periods of the history.   During the past three decades, however, biblical research has added so much to our knowledge that we have passed beyond the realm of that prophet's vision.

Renan, in his *History of the People of Israel,* so often abandons the scientific principles which he claims to champion, and states his own brilliant conjectures as if they were established facts, that his work is as untrustworthy as that of Edersheim.   The same criticism is applicable in a lesser degree to the historical narrative contained in Doctor Oort's *Bible for Learners.*

Although written half a century ago, the monumental work of Ewald shares with that of Stanley (which was largely founded upon it) the title of being the best single *History of Israel* in English.   This means, however, that these books can be profitably employed only as they are constantly supplemented by the results of subsequent discoveries.

Professor McCurdy, in his *History, Prophecy, and the Monuments,* has opened to general Bible students an exceedingly rich mine of material.   The field which this treatise covers is so wide that the reader gains an impression rather of the environment of the Hebrews than of their national life itself.   The former impression, however, is absolutely essential to a true appreciation of Israelitish history, and therefore the work is very useful for reference.

The biblical articles in the *Encyclopædia Britannica,* as is well known, were contributed by the leading Old and New Testament scholars of to-day, and contain the outlines of the most reliable history of the Hebrew people accessible to the general English reader.

The latest and in some ways most satisfactory historian of the Hebrew people is Professor Kittel.   While his methods are historical and critical, his positions are always as conservative as the facts will permit.   In the latter respect he differs radically from Stade, whose work is the most exhaustive *Geschichte des Volkes Israel* which has appeared since the days of Ewald.   Both Kittel and Stade base their conclusions upon a careful analysis of the sources, and consequently agree in the broad outlines.   Much valuable historical material is also to be found in Reuss' *Geschichte des Alten Testaments*.

A rich literature upon the religion of the Hebrews has sprung up since the historical methods of investigation have been generally adopted.   The works by the late Professor W. Robertson Smith are especially suggestive, even though one does not finally accept all his conclusions.   Fortunately for the English public, the admirable work by Professor Schultz has recently been translated from the fourth German edition.   While its spirit is temperate, it is also progressive, and embodies the results of a ripe scholarship.   The same progressive-conservative tone characterizes the volume of Hibbert Lectures by Montefiore on *The Religion of the Ancient Hebrews*.   The two latest volumes upon Old Testament theology both rest on historical and critical foundations, and are full of rich suggestion.   In their general positions, that of Dillman may be placed side by side with the history of Kittel, while the theology of Smend is based upon the conclusions of Wellhausen and Stade.

Next to Driver's *Introduction*, no book has appeared within the past decade which is as useful for all classes of Bible students as G. A. Smith's *Historical Geography of Palestine*.   Nowach's *Lehrbuch der Hebräischen Archäologie* contains a wealth of valuable facts, which unfortunately are not yet accessible in English.

BOOKS OF REFERENCE

LITERATURE

Abbreviations

Dri. . . . . . . Driver — Introduction to the Literature of the Old Testament, 1891.

Moore . . . . . Moore — Critical and Exegetical Commentary on Judges, 1895.

Cheyne . . . . Cheyne — Aids to the Devout Study of Criticism, 1892.

Hor. . . . . . . Horton — Revelation and the Bible (2d edition), 1893.

Kent . . . . . Kent — The Wise Men of Ancient Israel and their Proverbs, 1895.

Well. . . . . . Wellhausen — Prolegomena to the History of Israel, 1885.

Budde . . . . Budde — Die Bücher Richter und Samuel, 1890.

Corn. . . . . . Cornill — Einleitung in das Alte Testament (2te Aufl.), 1892.

HISTORY

Ew. . . . . . . Ewald — History of Israel, I.-III. (Eng. transl. 1883-1885).

McC. . . . . . McCurdy — History, Prophecy, and the Monuments, I. 1894.

En. B. . . . . Encyclopædia Britannica (Biblical articles).

Kitt. . . . . . Kittel — Geschichte der Hebräer, I. II. 1888, 1892.

Reuss. . . . . Reuss — Geschichte des Alten Testaments (2te Ausg.), 1890.

St. . . . . . . Stade — Geschichte des Volkes Israel, I. 1887.

RELIGION

Abbreviations

W. R. S. . . . Smith, W. R. — The Prophets of Israel, 1882.

Smith, R. S. . Smith, W. R. — The Religion of the Semites
(2d edition), 1894.

Schultz . . . . Schultz — Old Testament Theology, I. II. (Eng.
transl. 1892).

Mont. . . . . . Montefiore — The Religion of the Ancient Hebrews, 1892.

Dill. . . . . . Dillman — Handbuch der Alttestamentlichen
Theologie, 1895.

Smend . . . . Smend — Alttestamentliche Theologie, 1893.

ANTIQUITIES AND HISTORICAL GEOGRAPHY

G. A. S. . . . Smith, G. A. — The Historical Geography of the
Holy Land, 1894.

Con. . . . . . Conder — Tent Work in Palestine, 1887.

Now. . . . . . Nowack — Lehrbuch der Hebräischen Archäologie, I. II. 1894.

REFERENCES

PART I. — INTRODUCTORY STUDIES

I

SCOPE AND IMPORTANCE OF HEBREW HISTORY

Kitt. I. 3–6; Reuss, 2–7, 34; St. 1–12.

II

THE SOURCES OF HEBREW HISTORY

Jer. xviii. 18; Hor. 91–118; Kent, 11–31; Ew. I. 11–61, 157–163; McC. 13–15; En. B. III. 634–640, XIX. 814–821, 726–729, 880–882; Schultz, I. 14–31; Reuss, 8–30, 151–163; St. 12–41.

III

THE LAND OF THE HEBREWS

G. A. S. 3–28, 45–90, 127–571; W. R. S. 21–25; Con. 214–285; McC. 156, 157; Ew. 214–224; Kitt. I. 9–17; Reuss, 47–49; St. 100–113; Now. I. 25–90.

IV

THE ANCIENT TRIBES INHABITING PALESTINE

McC. 152–202, 22–24, 43–47, 73, 74, 406–408, 24, 25, 243–245; 203, 204, 234; En. B. IV. 763, 764, XVIII. 801–810, XXII. 822, XVIII. 755–757, XVI. 533–536, I. 742, 743, XII. 699; Ew. I. 224–255; W. R. S. 26–28; Kitt. I. 17–24; St. 113–124.

V

THE GENESIS OF THE HEBREW PEOPLE

En. B. XIII. 396-400, XXI. 641-643, XVI. 860, 861, XIX.
726, 727; Dri. 20-96; Hor. 60-90; Well. 295-362; Ew. I. 63-132,
300-423, II. 1-228; McC. 224-226; W. R. S. 32-37; Smith, R. S.
1-22, 28-139; Schultz, I. 86-139; Mont. 8-54; Kitt. I. 25-33,
43-281; Reuss, 35-16, 54-66, 71-104; St. 47-64, 124-133; Dill.
45-131; Smend, 12-48, 94-122; Now. I. 223-228, II. 1-7.

PART II. — SETTLEMENT IN CANAAN AND THE PREPARATION FOR THE UNITED KINGDOM

I

HISTORICAL SOURCES FOR THIS PERIOD

Judges and I. Samuel i.-vii. supplemented by Joshua and Ruth;
Dri. 151-164, 96-109, 425-428; En. B. XIII. 763, 764; Hor. 91-
100; Well. 228-248; Moore, Introd. xiii-xxxvii; Ew. I. 139-147;
Budde, 1-166; Corn. 86-106; Kitt. II. 3-25; St. 64-71.

II

SETTLEMENT AND FINAL LOCATION OF THE HEBREW TRIBES

Judges i. 1-7, 19-21, 10-18, 22-36; xvii. 1-xviii. 31 [cf. Josh.
xiii.-xix., which, though late, is suggestive]; McC. 224-230; En.
B. XIII. 400, 401, XVIII. 176; Ew. II. 274-310. 315-357; Kitt.
II. 55-59, 62-65; Reuss, 66-71, 104-117, 135; St. 133-173.

III

HEBREW CHAMPIONS AND WARS OF DELIVERANCE ·

Judges iii. 7-31; x. 1-5; xi. 1-xii. 15; xiii. 2-xvi. 31; iv. 4-
v. 31; McC. 55, 230-233; En. B. XIII. 401; Ew. II. 357-361, 373-
379, 392-408; G. A. S. 381-397; Kitt. II. 60-62, 65-69, 79-82;
Reuss, 125-128; St. 173-180.

IV

ORIGIN AND HISTORY OF THE KINGDOM OF GIDEON

Judges viii. 4-ix. 57 [cf. later narrative vi. 1-viii. 3]; En. B. XIII. 401; McC. 56, 231, 232; Ew. II. 379-392; Kitt. II. 69-79; Reuss, 128-131; St. 181-196.

V

THE PHILISTINE YOKE

I. Samuel i. 1-vii. 1; Jeremiah vii. 12, 14; xxvi. 6; McC. 236-238; En. B. XIII. 401; Con. 44-47; Ew. II. 413-419; Moore, Introd. xxxvii-xliii; Kitt. II. 91-94; St. 197-206.

VI

SOCIAL AND RELIGIOUS CONDITIONS DURING THE PERIOD OF THE JUDGES

Judges viii. 24-27 a; ix. 4; xiii. 5; xvii. 1-xviii. 31; I. Samuel iii. 1-vii. 1; Judges i. 7; iii. 15-23; viii. 31; ix. 1-5, 56, 57; xi. 30-40; xvi. 1; xix. 1-xxi. 25; I. Samuel ii. 12-26; Judges iii. 28; v. 2-8; ix. 23; xi. 21-27, 29; McC. 31-38, 52-55; En. B. XIII. 402; W. R. S. 31, 37-74; Schultz, I. 139-151; Smith, R. S. 140-212; Mont. 55-72; Kitt. II. 82-90; Dill. 131-142; Reuss, 137-143; Smend, 48-55, 61-63, 70-74, 130-151; Now. I. 228-250, 300-305, II. 7-25, 87-94, 203-216.

PART III. — HISTORY OF THE UNITED KINGDOM

I

HISTORICAL SOURCES

I. Samuel vii. 2-xxxi. 13; II. Samuel; I. Kings i. 1-xi. 43; I. Chronicles x.-xxix.; II. Chronicles i.-ix.; Song of Songs; Dri. 164-183, 484-502; 413-424; Hor. 101-108, 119-144, 205, 206; Kent, 41, 42; Well. 171-187, 249-285; Cheyne, 3-15; Ew. I.

136-139, 147-153, 164-168; En. B. XXI. 252, 253, VI. 837, XIV. 83-85; Budde, 167-276; Corn. 106-125; Kitt. II. 25-54; St. 71-75.

II

THE ESTABLISHMENT OF THE HEBREW KINGDOM

I. Samuel ix. 1-x. 16 ; xi. 1-15; xiii. 1-7, 16-23; xiv. 1-48, 52; En. B. XIII. 402, 403; McC. 55, 56; Con. 255, 256; W. R. S. 45, 47, 85, 389-391; Ew. III. 2-8, 15-28; Kitt. II. 94-104; Reuss, 181-184; St. 207-223.

III

THE DECLINE OF SAUL, AND THE RISE OF DAVID

I. Samuel xv. 1-35 [cf. xiii. 7-14]; xvi. 14-23 [cf. xvii. 1-xviii. 5; II. Samuel xxi. 19]; xviii. 6-xxx. 31; En. B. VI. 838, 839; Cheyne, 74-126; Con. 260-278; Ew. III. 29-48, 54-103; Kitt. II. 104-113; Reuss, 184-187; St. 223-252.

IV

THE BATTLE OF GILBOA, AND THE DEATH OF SAUL

I. Samuel xxxi. 1-13; McC. 241; En. B. XIII. 403, 404; G. A. S. 400-403; Ew. III. 48-53; Kitt. II. 114-119, 103-107; St. 253-257.

V

DAVID KING OVER JUDAH, AND THE FALL OF THE HOUSE OF SAUL

II. Samuel i. 1-iv. 12; En. B. XIII. 404; Ew. III. 107-119; Kitt. II. 120-130; Reuss, 188; St. 257-264.

VI

DAVID KING OVER ALL ISRAEL

II. Samuel v. 1-vii. 29; xxi. 18-22; xxiii. 8-23 ; Ew. III. 120-137; McC. 246; Con. 9; Kitt. II. 130-139; Reuss, 188-190; St. 265-270.

VII

DAVID'S FOREIGN WARS AND CONQUESTS

II. Samuel viii. 1-8; x. 1-xi. 1; xii. 26-31; I. Kings xi. 15-17; Psalm lx.; En. B. XIII. 404, 405; McC. 241-248; Ew. III. 137-160; Kitt. II. 139-143.

VIII

THE ORGANIZATION OF DAVID'S KINGDOM

II. Samuel v. 11; viii. 9, 10, 15-18; xx. 23-26; xxiii. 8-39; xxiv. 1-25; En. B. VI. 839, 840; Ew. III. 160-163; McC. 248, 249; Kitt. II. 144, 145; St. 273-279; Now. I. 305-314, 357-375.

IX

DAVID'S FAMILY HISTORY

II. Samuel iii. 2-5; xi. 1-xx. 22 ; En. B. VI. 840, 841; Ew. III. 163-195; McC. 249; Kitt. II. 145-151; St. 279-292.

X

THE CHARACTER AND WORK OF DAVID

En. B. VI. 836-841, XIII. 405 ; Cheyne, 16-73 ; Ew. III. 195-203; Kitt. II. 152; St. 295-299.

XI

THE ACCESSION OF SOLOMON

I. Kings i.-ii.; Ew. III. 204-216; Kitt. II. 153-158; St. 292-295.

XII

THE FOREIGN AND HOME POLICY OF SOLOMON

I. Kings 'xi. 14-25; iii. 1 ; v. 1-18; ix. 10-x. 29, iv. 1-34; iii. 16-28; Song of Songs iii.; I. Kings xi. 1-8; En. B. XIII. 405, XIX. 880 ; Kent, 58-62 ; McC. 250, 251; Ew. III. 216-225, 251-319; Kitt. II. 159-163; St. 299-311.

XIII

THE PALACE AND TEMPLE OF SOLOMON

I. Kings vi. 1–38; vii. 1–viii. 66 [cf. Ezekiel xl.–xlvi.]; En. B. XXIII. 166, 167; Con. 183–189; Ew. III. 226–251; Kitt. II. 164–169; St. 311–343; Now. II. 25–50.

XIV

SOCIAL AND RELIGIOUS CONDITIONS UNDER THE UNITED KINGDOM

Schultz, I. 151–157, 161–220; Well. 131–133; Mont. 72–83; Kitt. II. 169–176; Dill. 142–162; Smend, 55–59, 79–129; Now. II. 94–101.

A HISTORY

OF

THE HEBREW PEOPLE.

By CHARLES FOSTER KENT, Ph.D.

Professor of Biblical Literature and History
in Brown University.

Vol. I. THE UNITED KINGDOM. From the Settlement in Canaan to the Division of the Kingdom. $1.25 net.
Vol. II. THE DIVIDED KINGDOM. $1.25 net.

PERSONAL AND PRESS NOTICES.

WARREN H. LANGDON, *Professor of Practical Theology, San Francisco Theological Seminary.* — "This is a learned and ably written work. To those who adopt the conclusions of the Higher Criticism it will be a very acceptable history of the Hebrew People from their settlement in Canaan to the close of the united kingdom. It is written in an interesting, vigorous, and lucid style, easily grasped by the ordinary student."

GEORGE S. GOODSPEED, *Professor of Semitics, University of Chicago.* — "I believe that the book, on account of the excellence of its contents and the vividness and simplicity of its style, is by far the best history of the Hebrew People in English for Colleges and Bible teachers. I am persuaded that it will do a real service in broadening the mind and clarifying the knowledge of all into whose hands it may fall."

IRVING F. WOOD, *Professor of Biblical Literature, Smith College.* — "The book, with its brief chapters and popular style, is exactly what is needed now. The criticism, called new, though it is a generation old to the scholars, has made the Bible so much richer, and more valuable, that it needs to be reopened to the people. This reopening, such books as this of Professor Kent will do. It is very cautious in the statement of controverted points, but at the same time very clear where the results of scholarship are positive. Its study of the sources of Hebrew History and of the period of the Judges seems to me to be very valuable."

THE OUTLOOK. — "It is conceived and executed in the spirit of modern criticism: treats the history and literature of Israel as history and literature, but is wholly reverent in its tone and constructive in its purpose; an excellent text-book for the study of Old Testament history."

THE CHRISTIAN ADVOCATE. — "The whole volume presents a rare combination of graphic delineation and careful accuracy in regard to historic fact. Used in connection with the Bible only, it must prove most valuable to the ordinary reader, while if studied with a use of the authorities named in the appendix, it will be a firm and solid stepping-stone into a vast and important region of knowledge not yet fully explored or bounded."

THE CONGREGATIONALIST. — "It purposely avoids argument, and gives a clear picture of the development of the Hebrew Nation in accordance with the views of the modern critics. The author closely follows their results, and any criticism of the book would necessarily involve that of the whole school. The great body of modern scholars now hold this position, and instruction therein is provided for in many of our colleges. This book is especially fitted for a reference and text-book for such classes."

METHODIST REVIEW. — "We have seldom read a small book which has so much of clearly stated, well-wrought, and inspiring matter packed into its pages. Whether an instructor should accept or reject its methods and conclusions, we doubt if a better book could be found for the instruction of college classes.

CHARLES SCRIBNER'S SONS,

153-157 Fifth Avenue, - - - **NEW YORK.**